Trappers
&
Trailblazers

Caitlin Press Inc.
8100 Alderwood Road,
Halfmoon Bay, BC V0N 1Y1
www.caitlin-press.com

Text design by Teresa Karbashewski.
Cover design by Vici Johnstone.
Cover photograph courtesy Stan Simpson.

Printed in Canada.

Caitlin Press Inc. acknowledges financial support from the Government of
Canada through the Book Publishing Industry Development Program and
the Canada Council for the Arts, and from the Province of British Columbia
through the British Columbia Arts Council and the Book Publisher's Tax Credit.

Library and Archives Canada Cataloguing in Publication

Boudreau, Jack, 1933-
    Trappers and trailblazers / Jack Boudreau.

ISBN 978-1-894759-39-7

    1. Pioneers–British Columbia–Biography.
    2. Frontier and pioneer life–British Columbia.
    3. British Columbia–History–20th century. I. Title.

FC3817.3.B68 2009   971.1009'9   C2009-905592-9

TRAPPERS
&
TRAILBLAZERS

JACK BOUDREAU

CAITLIN PRESS

This book is dedicated to all people who do their part to keep the memories of the pioneers alive for future generations. I feel quite strongly that we can never do enough to repay what they went through to make life easier for all who followed in their footsteps. So to those who sit down and record the memories of your parents, you are doing your part to keep a record for others to enjoy somewhere along the trail of life.

It pleases me a great deal to note that more and more people are taking an interest in local history, and that it is becoming more popular with each passing year.

—Jack Boudreau

CONTENTS

INTRODUCTION

In this, my seventh book, I have endeavored to cover a variety of different subjects. Although most of these stories concern the woods, I have strayed from adventures in the wild with the Ward family story which involved a daring trip across Canada by automobile during the early forties when money was scarce. The entire family, including children, played in a band and people were so impressed that they readily handed out money to help with the expenses even though they had little for themselves. Aside from that story, I have once again written about my favourite subject—adventures on the rivers and in the mountains of BC.

Of all the people I have met and interviewed, few have impressed me as much as the Perry family, who have lived at their ranch along the Willow River since their father purchased the property in 1914. The oldest surviving Perry, John, is a person who should be an inspiration to people with disabilities. As a young man, he suffered a broken back and severe head injuries. After toughing it out through three years of medical treatment in Vancouver, he returned home wheelchair-bound for life. John made a promise not to be a burden on others, and he kept that promise by repeatedly doing the seemingly impossible. The first winter following his return, John bucked and split sixty cords of firewood, which was readily sold in Prince George. As I was to witness several years later, he tied himself in his wheelchair so he couldn't fall out and then went to work with a power saw or axe. The Perry story is one that

I feel proud to present and I am honored that I have been given their permission to do so.

Once again I lucked out by obtaining several journals recorded many years ago by people who thoughtfully put pen to paper while travelling our northern wilderness. Some settled the Interior of British Columbia during the first half of the twentieth century, while others came here in search of gold or furs and then left the area, often without hitting the motherlode. This book contains many highlights from these journals that I have been fortunate enough to gain access to. Even though hardships and sorrow were often the norm, these people experienced such memorable adventures that they looked back with satisfaction, not the least regretful of what they went through. What shows up time and again is that most of these people possessed an intangible mettle and sense of humor that saw them through the rough spots. One elderly lady who was a well-known taxidermist in the Interior for about forty years, summed up the lives of the people she knew by saying, "Sure, people faced some bad times, but isn't it true that after the worst storms we find the most beautiful rainbows?"

I hope readers will understand the repeat of a couple stories that I used in previous books. My reason for doing so is because new information came to my attention. This is especially true with "Conspiracy of Silence," a story that has intrigued me for most of my lifetime. Imagine my surprise when going through the archives to find a picture of William Goodson who was murdered along the Torpy River in 1926. The murder was never solved, and perhaps rightfully so if he was a fur thief as charged.

Most of these adventures took place in the northern half of this province, which is understandable because it has such a rich history. Many times I find the same names permeating the wilderness; showing just how insatiable their appetite was for constant adventure. It is my sincere wish that readers will enjoy the results of the endless hours I spent researching these stories.

—Jack Boudreau

Willow River Canyon.

A Day
to Remember

Edwin Perry was born in Beardstown, Illinois, and later moved to Spokane, Washington, where he owned and operated a shoe store for a time. During that time their first-born son was lost because of an inability to digest food. In search of a change, Edwin lost interest in the store when he learned that a new railway was being constructed through central British Columbia. Along with his wife, Frances, he moved to Tete Jaune, eighty-five kilometres (fifty-three miles) west of the Alberta boundary, where he was employed as a cement engineer for the Grand Trunk Pacific Railway.

During that summer of 1912, Edwin was at Tete Jaune when a group of men arrived there looking for work with the railroad. When informed that the railway was not hiring, the men took off walking toward Fort George. Sometime later, relatives in California notified the police in Fort George that they had not been contacted by these men and so a search was started that produced no trace whatsoever. The only plausible explanation was that the men had built a raft and drifted into the whirlpool in the Grand Canyon located 171 kilometres (106 miles) upriver of Fort George. This is but one of many stories alluding to the tremendous loss of life in the Grand Canyon during railway construction.

During the summer of 1912, Edwin was transferred to Fort George (later named Prince George) to help construct the new bridge across the Fraser River. Two years later, he was present when an elderly man drifted down the Fraser River on a raft. The man was able to paddle his raft to shore at Hospital Creek on the Willow River but it was apparent that he was suffering from scurvy and extreme starvation. Edwin assisted in getting him to the hospital where it was discovered that this man carried two quart jars full of gold. Although quizzed as to the location of the gold source, the man remained silent and took the secret to the grave with him just a short time later.

With the completion of the cement work surfacing tunnels, culverts and bridges, Edwin was offered a similar job in China, which he refused. He was fed up with living in boxcars and the like. Instead, because he liked the fish and game so abundant in the Interior, he moved his wife and two children, Lila and Miles, into a small house in Fort George. After a short search, he purchased a 160-acre parcel of land along the Willow River, thirty kilometres (nineteen miles) east of Fort George.

Edwin's wife, Frances Goddard, learned what it was like to be a pioneer's child in the American West. She was just twelve years old when their family started out by covered wagon from Kentucky to Illinois; a move that spanned over two years with stopovers during the winter months. The buffaloes (bison) were being slaughtered at that time and that led to starvation among the Native people. In an attempt to get food, they raided the wagon train. As practiced, the family moved the wagons into a circle, and the cattle and horses were placed inside to prevent the Natives from taking them. When the battle began, the children and women were kept busy re-loading rifles for the men, as they had been trained to do. During the battle, one Native breached the circle and was attacking one of the defenders when Frances shot and killed him. The attack was driven off, but Frances carried the burden of killing a fellow human throughout her lifetime. John told me that it was almost impossible to get her to talk about it as she would always say that it made her sick to think of it. As was often the case among remote pioneers, Frances served as midwife whenever her services were required.

With his transition to the life of rancher, Edwin purchased a fine team of matched black horses for $500. An enormous sum of money at the time, especially when we consider the fact that men were working the railway grade for two dollars per twelve-hour day. This puts the true value of the horses into perspective.

During May 1916, Edwin was living in a tent on the new property clearing land. One morning, May 14th, he went to harness the horses only to find that they ran away at his approach. Edwin gathered some food and supplies and started trailing the horses along the Willow River, as losing his horses was a financial loss he could not bear. He trailed the horses all along the river and up to Bowron Lake and adjacent country. All through the summer he followed them, living off the land by eating berries, fish, grouse and rabbits or whatever else he could find of an edible nature. At times he got right close to the horses, but was never able to get a rope on them. Finally the snows of the approaching winter drove him out of the mountains and he arrived at civilization in the town of Barkerville, where he contacted the police. They informed him that a cowboy had captured his two horses just a few days earlier and taken them out of the area. Forced to give up on the horses, Edwin walked to Quesnel and caught the last sternwheeler of the season back to Prince George. The date was November 27th. He had been gone six and a half months. When he arrived home sporting a heavy beard, his wife, having given him up for dead, mistook him for a beggar until he spoke to her.

After the railway was completed, a downturn in the economy took place. Among the businesses that went under were two of the early-day merchants in Prince George—Kennedy and Blair, who were forced into bankruptcy. Edwin purchased their supplies and moved them out to the new property, intending to sell the supplies off piecemeal. His plan failed, sadly, because people helped themselves to his goods whenever his back was turned.

Many of the pre-emptors (homesteaders) that had purchased land along the Willow River had done so because the new railroad was to pass through that area just a short distance below the Willow Canyon. At the same time, another rumour suggested that the railway was to cross the McGregor River and follow the north bank of the Fraser to Fort (Prince) George. I believe the railway deliberately spread these rumors to cause confusion and prevent people from buying the land and then reselling it to the railway for huge profits. When the railroad switched to the Giscome shortcut, many of these people put up their land for sale. Over several years, the Perrys purchased much of the adjacent acreage, which they own to this day.

The Perry family was completed in 1918 with the arrival of John, and throughout his youth he quickly learned the ways of the wild. As for education, the two boys received limited schooling by boarding in Prince George for several years.

Their days on the ranch were often exciting, such as the day the two lads were chased by their bull when they attempted to bring the cattle home for milking. Things came to a head just a short time later when Edwin was attacked and severely injured by this same bull. For three weeks he was confined to bed with some broken ribs and other wounds. As soon as he got back on his feet the bull ended up in the stew pot.

Edwin supplied proof that all men were not honest and above board in a story he told his sons. A Native trapper came to their ranch with three hundred beaver pelts that he had obtained along the Willow River. Edwin took the man and his furs into Prince George the following day and agreed to meet him the next morning for the return trip home. Upon leaving Edwin, the trapper took his furs to a fur buyer who gave him a few dollars and said, "Come back later today for the money after I've had time to evaluate the furs." When the trapper returned late that day with a belly full of booze, the fur buyer told him he had already paid him all the money. The poor chap had to borrow a few dollars from Edwin to get tobacco for the trip home. He returned to his cabin without any food. Edwin claimed that this was not an isolated incident; some dishonest fur buyers knew that if their clients got drunk, they could tell them that they had paid them in full and convince the trappers that they had forgotten this and lost the money somehow. Apparently many trappers were cheated in this manner.

John experienced similar dealings with fur buyers. He recalls the time he shot three coyotes and skinned them out as fur. He took them to a fur buyer in Prince George and the haggling began. The best offer was three dollars, which John refused. He then stated flat out that he would not take a penny under five dollars. Apparently the song and dance that followed was something to behold. The buyer pulled his hair and shouted, "You are breaking me; I will have nothing left." It took a while, but John's offer was finally accepted.

John related a tale of sorrow he heard from his mother, a tragedy that took place along the Willow River in 1919. The Spanish flu was terrorizing the world at that time and the Native people were especially susceptible to it. In an effort to escape what was ravaging their populations, a group of sixteen Natives left their reserve at Shelley and set up a tent camp on Spey Creek about one and half kilometres (one mile) from its confluence with the Willow River. One or two of the men would visit the Perry Ranch every three or four days to pick up food such as milk, eggs and potatoes. On one occasion Edwin heard gunshots coming from the direction of their camp but thought they were just hunting game. When they didn't show at the ranch for over a week, Edwin walked to their camp where he was in for a heartbreaking surprise; a moose was standing in the centre of their camp and all around it lay the bodies of the Natives. None survived. Edwin notified the authorities and a short time later three men came from Shelley in a dugout and carried all the bodies from the camp to the Willow River where they built a temporary camp. That night one of the attending Natives died, again a victim of the flu. Over the next few days the remaining two men constructed a large raft with which they moved all the bodies down the Willow and Fraser rivers to Prince George where they were interred in the Native graveyard near the Hudson's Bay store.

During the 1920s Edwin suffered a great deal from ulcers. There were three physicians in Prince George at that time, but none familiar with treating ulcers. In desperation, the family searched for help and a promise of help came from a doctor in Calgary, Alberta. In 1927 Edwin arrived at the hospital where his condition was assessed. The doctor informed the family that Edwin was too weak to undergo surgery. He passed away a short time later.

This left Miles at age thirteen and John, age nine, to take care of the farm and assist their mother. Both boys quit school and became rancher/farmers. John did not regret his lack of schooling; in fact he stated, "I think I have learned more during my years on the ranch than if I had stayed in school my entire life."

Sometimes the boys performed chores that seemed beyond their years. For instance, a neighbour named Pickering was extremely allergic to the glycerin in blasting powder so John, barely out of childhood, earned a few dollars by doing his blasting work for him. This powder was absolutely necessary for blowing out stumps during land clearing. The powder was relatively cheap at the time and on occasion miners would donate whatever powder they could spare. The following years were tough as the Great Depression came upon them. As John put it, "We worked damned hard but we never went hungry."

The family named Pickering lived upriver several miles from the Perry Ranch. The only means of access to and from their cabin was by crossing the Willow River and then following the Perry Road to Prince George. This meant that they could cross the river when the water level was low or walk on the ice when it was strong enough to hold the weight of the horses. One winter day they had attempted to cross on the ice only to have the horse break through into three feet of water. Mr. Pickering came to the Perry's for assistance and they spent the better part of the day trying in vain to get the horse out of the ice. After a great deal of hard work they chopped a trench through the ice from the horse to shore and managed to get the poor beast out. John pointed out that they assisted many people through the years and I surely believe him.

John told another story about their neighbour, Pickering.

Sue Walker and Miles Perry with his daughter, Esther.

Apparently he got bit on the back of his hand by what he thought was a snake. When he arrived at the Perry Ranch a few days later his forearm was swollen and terribly infected. John's mother made a poultice out of bread and milk and applied it to the infected area and overnight the swelling disappeared. As John put it, "Garter snakes are not poisonous but something sure got into his arm."

When Edwin first purchased the ranch, there was a trail worn into the ground fifteen to twenty centimetres (six to eight inches) deep from the Natives and pioneer woodsmen that travelled the area. Called the Dolimar Trail, it led out toward the Bear (Bowron) River and then turned south to Barkerville. When Miles and John were just lads, a Native worked for their father on the ranch. He told them that when he was a young lad a man called Cataline hired him to help with a pack train to Barkerville, which he did. This man claimed that he stayed on with the pack trains until Cataline retired. Regrettably, no date was mentioned, leaving the possibility that his first trip with Cataline may have taken place in the 1870s or '80s. Traces of the trail to Barkerville were still in evidence in the 1930s when John and Miles ran pack trains through the upper Willow/Bowron River area. They found where large fir trees had been chopped out with axes many years earlier.

John recalls the time he was falling trees when he found a rope inside the tree about ten metres (thirty-three feet) above ground level. The tree had grown completely around the rope that was still sound, having been protected from the weather. On another occasion they found a .22 rifle leaning against a tree with sap coated over the barrel. It had been there for many years and had been protected from the weather by the coating of pitch. A good deal of elbow grease managed to restore it to a like-new condition.

John described just how tough things were for many families during the Depression. An example was the plight of his neighbours, the Pickerings. They had about fifteen children and since there was no school in the area, they were forced to pack up and relocate to the Mud River area, west of Prince George, where their children had access to a school. This was but one of many families that were forced to relocate for any number of reasons. Many of these people had little to look forward to and nothing to look back on.

An adventure that could never be forgotten occurred in 1934, during spring high water, while the river was running hog wild.

Miles and John had purchased a purebred bull that cost them a pretty penny, to put it mildly. The bull somehow managed to break out of its pen, and then slowly sauntered over to the river, where it stood for several minutes as though in deep thought. Suddenly it took a mighty leap out into the flood-swollen river. Miles and John followed along the riverbank and watched in horror as the bull went under a huge logjam the stretched across the river. Both men were certain that the bull had drowned, so they were astounded to see it come up below the logjam, blowing water and fighting for survival. Again it drifted down river and went under another log-jam. Once again the bull came up and managed to climb out on a small island near the opposite side of the river.

Both men were at a loss about what to do. There was no pos-sible way they wanted the bull to try swimming back across the river, so what to do? After two days had passed, it became obvi-ous that the bull was without feed and weakening. Finally the two men took their horses on the long trail around by Willow River to Giscome where they hit Hubbard Road. This was a one-way distance of about forty kilometres (twenty-five miles). In turn they followed this road to the river, a spot about five kilometres (three miles) downriver from where the bull was trapped. At this point they left their horses.

When the men tried to follow an old corduroy road along the river, they found the logs all afloat in the remaining snow and floodwater. Several hours later they arrived at the spot where the bull was standing, and realized that they had to force the bull across a large stream to get it off the island. The bull refused to cross, so this forced the men to fall two large cottonwood trees and build a bridge. By this time it was dark, so Miles lit and carried a lantern to lead the way. The bull refused to budge. Next the men stretched out the rope they had brought along, but found it was a few feet short of spanning the stream. Again the men improvised by using Miles' coveralls to join the rope to a tree. When Miles pulled on the rope, John gave the bull's tail a hard twist, to get it moving. Again the bull did the unpredictable and jumped over the side of the bridge where it was caught by the current and carried downstream.

With a great deal of effort, the men got the bull up the bank and then fought the floating corduroy logs all the way back to where the horses were tied. This meant that they had spent about ten hours in the water and snow. Totally exhausted, the men built a large campfire, had tea and lunch and then slept for several hours. The following day they returned the long way around to the ranch. John states that they made certain the bull could not escape from the second heavy-duty pen they placed him in.

During the Dirty Thirties, John and Miles spent some time prospecting for gold around the Willow Canyon where they earned up to three dollars a day. Not the bonanza by any means, but as John puts it, "It was money we didn't have before."

I pursued the prospecting issue and John related a story about a Native that used to trap the upper river in winter, and then prospect the river during the summer. Several times he stopped at their ranch and showed them nuggets, some of which were the size of a fingernail. Apparently the Native was showing his poke in Prince George one day when a stranger offered him a deal. If he were shown the spot where the nuggets came from, he would give the Native a sleeping bag and a supply of groceries. The deal was struck. A few days later the man was taken to the bottom of the Willow Canyon where he set up his sluice box. Over the rest of the summer that man took 35 ounces (992 grams) of gold out of the

Esther and John Perry.

river and returned to Vancouver with a sizeable stake.

During one of their trips along the river, Miles and John found where men had dug a vertical shaft down thirty metres (ninety-eight feet) from a ridge to water level. The shaft was lined with poles and was over two metres (twenty-two feet) square. Not a trace of mineral could be found at the site and John states that they were at a loss to explain the enormous amount of effort that had been expended for no apparent reason.

One of John's stories may be of interest to prospectors. When he was a lad some of his Native friends told him that their parents used to go somewhere behind the Willow Canyon to a spot where they gathered lead. They used to chop it out with an axe, and then take it home where they molded it into bullets for use in their rifles. Since the Natives used to trap the entire river, "somewhere behind the Willow Canyon" covered an enormous amount of territory and nothing resembling lead was ever found to the best of their knowledge.

On another trip, Miles and John found a large pile of pipe about ten centimetres (four inches) in diameter. These pipes were located about thirty kilometres (nineteen miles) upriver of the canyon. Again, the men had no knowledge of the pipes' purpose.

During the early years on the ranch, Miles and John ran pack horses for the Forest Service, aiding them in mining, surveying and other ventures. Many times they were called out to fight wildfires. One fire was particularly memorable because of the huge man that was brought along as cook. To get to this fire, they had to ford the Bowron River. The so-called chef refused to cross, so they loaded him on a pack horse and started across the river. About halfway across, the horse fell and the man ended up floating down the river. He made no attempt to swim and would surely have drowned had not the men run out and pulled him to shore. Many times during that fire these men cursed themselves for rescuing him. An example of their complaints was the time some of the men caught a good supply of fish and handed them to the cook to prepare for dinner. When the men went to eat, they found all the fish had been fried with the heads on and the entrails intact. One of the men expressed his view of the meal by stating, "I refuse to eat anything that is staring at me."

Prior to the arrival of the Grand Trunk Pacific Railway in Prince

George, several pioneer types took out homesteads along the Willow River in anticipation of the railway crossing their area and paying good dollars for their land. When the railway went a different direction, these men sold out or just gave up and left. One such man was Jim Johnson who owned property where Spey Creek runs into the Willow River. In later years Jim spent about twenty years on the island under the Fraser River Bridge where he kept a herd of goats. Just how he managed to survive is not clear, unless perhaps he sold goat milk in the area. What is memorable about his time on the island occurred during World War Two when three guards were posted on the bridge. One evening Jim decided to go into town for some revelry. He ascended a ladder onto the bridge and walked right into one of the guards. Caught completely by surprise, the guard assumed that the bridge was under attack. He later told the Perry family that Jim had came within a hair of meeting his maker.

Jim Johnson with sturgeon caught off Goat Island, July 12, 1913.
COURTESY THE EXPLORATION PLACE P981.19.56

John recalls that back in 1933 Jim landed a huge sturgeon with a one-inch rope and a chicken for bait. This fish was displayed in Billy Monroe's butcher shop on Third Avenue. It was immensely impressive in that the head touched the ceiling and the tail was on the floor. A winch truck had to be taken out on the bridge in order to lift the monster fish up off the island. A short time later, also beside the island, Jim caught another sturgeon that broke the one-inch-thick rope.

Perhaps the most memorable event of their lives started in the mid-thirties when a young lady named Margaret Goddard started teaching school at Ferndale about thirteen kilometres (eight miles) from the ranch. Miles started dating her and just a few years later she moved back to Trail, BC. John recalls that it was during the summer of 1938 that Miles went to visit her. A short time later, Miles notified John that he and Margaret were going to be wed. Further, they wanted him to drive to Trail and be best man. John scouted around and found a reliable man to take care of the ranch and planned his journey. First off, he tried on his old suit that had not been worn for many years. The pant legs were much too short and the buttons with their respective button holes on the vest and jacket couldn't even approach each other, let alone hook up. John took the suit to a tailor in Prince George where he explained his problem, and the tailor agreed to make the corrections. The next day John picked up the suit and started on the two-day drive to Trail. He arrived in Trail early in the morning and rather than be a bother to anyone, he got a motel room and retired for a much-needed sleep.

When John awoke, he got cleaned up and attempted to put on the altered suit. The pants and vest fit fine, but when he tried to put on the jacket, he found that the tailor had put one sleeve in backwards. What to do? With the wedding only a few hours away, John went searching for a tailor and finally found a Chinese shop where he hoped he could get some emergency repairs. The man refused, outright, and they had a mean session going for a time.

Perry family: John, Lyla, Francis and Miles, 1945. COURTESY JOHN PERRY

John was at the point of threatening him when he finally conceded and redid the sleeve. With the altered jacket on his body, John arrived at the church just as the wedding was getting underway.

After the wedding, Miles and Margaret left on a honeymoon trip to the US, while John attended a party with a group of people he neither knew nor had anything in common with. "They were miners and I was a rancher so we had absolutely nothing in common. The solution—John got back in his vehicle and spent another two days on the road back to Prince George.

It was during the summer of 1940 that two men arrived at the Perry Ranch. Both claimed to be geologists employed by the Provincial Government. They wanted to hire John with five pack horses to take them along the Willow River to the area of Bowron Lake where they had work to perform. A price was agreed upon and they proceeded on their journey. This trail located on the west side of the Willow River had been constructed by the Forest Service so they would have access to a huge area of forest, replete with virgin stands of timber. Crews were hired on occasion to build bridges across sloughs and streams.

On this journey, it didn't take long for John to realize that these men were bush-dumb. An example was when they would hit an old burn. Instead of skirting it, the men insisted on cutting trail through the burn—a time-consuming and unnecessary job. Several times they almost got into fisticuffs over similar decisions. At last they reached an area near the Bowron Lakes where they appeared to be looking at rocks in the creek. By that time John was suspicious that these men were not working for the government, rather they were exploring on their own. After a few days on the stream, the men asked him to unload their supplies and return for them in a few weeks. John asked for his pay but was told he would receive it in due time from Victoria. When he went to gather some food for the return trip, they told him that there was not any food to spare so he should take an extra day and go to Barkerville for food. John informed these men that he had no money with him, and since they refused to assist him financially, he left for home without any food.

The first day on the trail, he managed to kill a grouse with a rock and that was his daily food intake. The second evening, he came to a deserted mining camp. The tables were set but the place was filthy from packrat droppings. All John found to eat was some dried apples and syrup, which he readily devoured. Two more days were spent on the trail without food except for a porcupine that he attempted to roast over a campfire. Probably because of the food it ate, it was not fit for human consumption and he reached home without any further sustenance. A few weeks later when it was time to return for the men, it started snowing. This was all the excuse John needed to get out of the return trip. He never received a cent nor heard from the men thereafter.

During the years he spent packing, John enjoyed his memories of the mountains the most. He loved to play hide-and-seek with marmots, trying to sneak up on them. Without exception, the posted guards always spotted him and a shrill whistle sent the others to the safety of their lairs.

When queried about problems encountered in packing John offered, "I think one of the most difficult things we ever packed was planed lumber. No matter how carefully it was packed, it always managed to slide out and had to be repacked again and again. Another tough thing to carry was an eighteen-foot canoe that we tied on two horses. The rear horse was almost completely blindfolded so it had no choice but to follow the lead horse."

John broke many horses throughout his youth, including wild horses captured in the Chilcotin area. They developed a rather clever method of breaking horses by starting them out with a blindfold on and a short rope from their halter to the saddle horn of another horse. This meant the horse was unable to buck. The second day they would put a heavier load on the horse and so on until it got used to the loads.

John had an encounter with one wild bronco that he never forgot. Several times it reared up to throw him, but each time he held on. At last it threw itself over backwards and the saddle horn landed on John's shoulder causing a serious injury. When John finally got around to riding it again, it threw itself upside down and John narrowly escaped getting crushed. He immediately took a stick and hit the horse right between the eyes and knocked it cold; he had reached the point where he didn't care if he killed it. Many times after that he rode this same horse and not once did it ever buck again.

When the Perrys left the pack train business, they got a riverboat and motor that gave them access to parts of the river. Again they were frequently called upon to take firefighters to fires along the river. Often this was scary business in that they had to be on the watch for logjams and rocks. After several scares, they got rid of the boat and motor and the forestry found other less dangerous ways of getting to their wildfires.

John believes it was late winter 1943 when he got a surprise visitor. Miles had taken his wife to Trail to visit her relatives and John was alone making breakfast when he saw a Native man coming on the run. As soon as he entered the house he blurted out that his wife was trying to give birth and had been in labour for a day and a night. He pleaded with John to come with him and give assistance. John refused, stating that he was not a doctor and could be charged if anything went wrong. The Native insisted that John had delivered lots of calves and there really wasn't that much difference. They considered the time it would take to try to get medical assistance from Prince George and the man assured John that she would not live that long.

At last John agreed and followed the man for five kilometres (three miles) through waist-deep snow to a tent out in the forest. It didn't take long for him to realize that the baby was upside-down. He corrected it and the baby arrived at once. Next, John got some water heated and cleaned both mother and baby. The final act for the day was when he noticed the mother's breasts were leaking milk, so he handed her the baby and immediately it began to feed. The father was only about eighteen years of age and living in a filthy tent with the mother and baby. Things got better for them the following year when they moved to Fort St. James. John got a letter from him saying that he had a job falling for an area sawmill. That was the last he heard of them so he guessed everything worked out alright.

When I asked John if he was aware of any fatalities in the Willow River besides the eight young men who perished at the canyon in 1972, he related a rather sad tale about an elderly man and his teenage son who prospected the river in 1935. These men brought a rickety boat and motor to the Perry Ranch, where they launched and headed downriver about fifteen kilometres (nine miles). They built a cabin at that spot which was near some logjams and a whirlpool, and then they set about prospecting. Tragedy struck when the young lad went to start the outboard motor. When he pulled the starter rope, it broke and he fell over the side of the boat into the river. Immediately below that spot sat a whirlpool and that is where his body got lodged. The father walked upriver to the Perry Ranch and asked for John's assistance. They searched the river for many hours but to no avail.

Several times in the following two weeks, the father arrived at their ranch to beseech John to assist in getting his son's body, which he thought he could see out in the river. A few times they went at night and this was a hairy experience trying to avoid the rocks and logjams with little light. Things came to a head one evening when the father arrived in a state of panic and told John that he had seen his son's body out in the river. He pleaded with John to take the boat down to the cabin area, but John refused because it was too dark. John told the father that he would be on the way downriver at first light and the man hurried away back toward his cabin. When John arrived at their cabin the next morning, he found it empty. A cold stove suggested that the father had not made it home the previous night. John set out along the trail toward the ranch and came upon his body lying in the trail. He had suffered heart failure.

John notified the police and the next morning they arrived at the ranch and went downriver to the spot where John had found the father's body. With a great deal of effort, they packed the body to the boat and took it to Prince George. The following day the police notified John that he should return to the cabin and pick up all the prospector's personal effects, which he did. Just as he was about to leave, he glanced out into the whirlpool to see the young lad's body floating amid the debris. Uncertain as to what action to take, he tied the body to shore and returned to the ranch to make another phone call to the police. Again the police returned to get the body. When they left, they asked John to return to the cabin the following day to tow the boat and motor back to the ranch. John did not relish the thought of trying to tow that tippy boat through the rocks and rapids, and as it turned out he didn't have to. By a stroke of luck or design, the rope had worn through and the boat had drifted away downriver; probably for the good of all. John claims that was his last trip downriver. In retrospect, John admits that the father's death bothered him a great deal as he felt responsible in part for his death. For whatever it was worth, I told him that I would have refused the night trip as well. Certainly two more deaths would have solved nothing.

When I asked John about other events that took place along the river, he replied, "If that river could talk it would have a million stories to tell; such as prospectors that went up the river and never returned. Perhaps they went out to civilization by a different route but there was no certain way to know what became of them."

Another example of trouble along the lower river occurred when two miners were hauling their supplies downriver. They came round a sharp curve to behold a cottonwood tree across the river right in front of them. Several pumps and other mining supplies were among the boat's contents and all of it was lost when the boat rolled. The two men washed up on a small island in the centre of the stream, but could not get to shore because the river was wild from the heavy fall rains. The next day Miles and John, who were expecting them, felt something was amiss because the men were overdue. They did not have a boat at that time but they walked upriver and found the trapped men. They felled a large cottonwood which hung up on the island and the men were effectively rescued. John said he knew of four rifles that were lost in the river; none were recovered.

A rather unusual individual named Thomas McCarthy lived three kilometres (two miles) west of the Perry Ranch back in the twenties. He would come to their home and sit in silence for hours. If Mrs. Perry offered cinnamon buns or other goodies to him, he would say, "I'll take them but I don't think I will eat them."

Thomas McCarthy had left a wife in Illinois and arrived in Prince George where he intended to open a machine shop. At every opportunity he would pack all manner of junk to his property where he lived in a small cabin. Many times he got Edwin to haul large pieces of equipment to his place, all of which Edwin considered junk. John described Thomas as a grouchy old man who had amazing abilities. For instance, he somehow managed to drag large logs out of the forest to his proposed machine shop. At the time that he perished from a bout of pneumonia, he had four rounds of logs up on his shop. Since this man had neither machinery nor horses, the mystery of how he moved the one-ton logs was never solved. This was but one of many things that he never shared with

Employee Debbie and John Perry.

others. He suffered terribly from rheumatism, and he used to keep two five-gallon cans of hot water in bed with him; he swore it helped.

Thomas had a rather strange belief that eating bear meat would improve his eyesight; consequently he was forever setting traps to get these animals. About twenty years after his death, Miles and John were punching a road into the area for logging purposes when they heard a chain rattle. They looked about in the thicket and came upon a black bear in a trap. The trap was jammed full of leaves and vegetation and was just holding the bear by two claws. John tied a hand axe to a pole and cut the bear free, while Miles covered it with his rifle. The bear made no attempt to bother the men—instead it moved away for a short distance and climbed a tree. The bear survived, but the biggest surprise was still to come, for the men found two more set bear traps in the same general area.

Sometimes when Edwin was going to town for supplies he would ask Thomas if he needed anything and his answer was always that he had everything he needed. It appeared that he subsisted on bannock, moose meat and bear meat. Thomas was an odd man indeed.

When the Perrys visited Prince George, they frequently ate in the CNR Café on Third Avenue. This café was owned by an oriental gentleman named Joe Sing, who, in turn, was friends with a fellow countryman that owned a dairy at Wells, BC. Through this connection, it was agreed that the Perrys would supply the Wells' man with forty tons of hay. Five trips were made at two tons per trip, a big load for their truck. In return they received the pay for the first ten tons, and then hauled the other thirty tons. On their last trip, they expected to be paid the balance, but they arrived to find that the sheriff had closed the place the previous day. This was a terrible loss during the hard times of the 1933. When all was said and done they did not get a cent for the other thirty tons.

During the early forties, a large number of cottonwood trees came downriver and plugged the river channel just adjacent to the ranch house. After many futile attempts to remove the jam which was washing their land away, the Perrys appealed to the Department of Highways for assistance. A series of wings were constructed to prevent the continual erosion of the farm, but they failed their objective. When the ice went out the following spring it took the wings along with it. At last the Perrys took matters into their own hands. They took their two tractors, a TD14A and a RD6 out into the river and pushed the tree-jam a considerable distance to where it would present no more problems.

All went well until a helicopter carrying fisheries personnel flew by and spotted the Cat tracks in the river. The chopper landed and the Perrys were questioned. John's answer was adequate, "The Department of Highways fooled around with that jam for a long time, so I guess it must have been them." Nothing further was ever mentioned about the incident and the erosion of their farmland stopped.

While I'm on the subject of cottonwood trees, I must mention that John added an interesting bit of trivia when he told me that they used cottonwood bark to heat their forge when coal was hard to get. I have never heard this from any other source.

Perhaps the strangest man to frequent the Willow River area during the 1940s, was a man named Con Moller who had a cabin and homestead near the Giscome area. This man trusted the Perry family and visited them on occasion. During the winter months Con would earn money by cooking for camps; much of this money was spent buying powder which he used to build a shaft into a hillside. Con claimed he was following a vein that could take him to the motherlode. On one occasion Con took Miles and John to the back end of this shaft. It was a spooky trip to say the least, as Con had dug under big boulders which could have collapsed and plugged the tunnel at any moment. John states that he was certainly happy to see the light of day after that venture. He also states that they saw nothing of interest as far as prospecting goes. He recalls the time two geologists crawled to the back of that shaft; they too spotted nothing of interest. Try to imagine the endless work that it took to build a shaft 100 metres (328 feet) into the mountain. Con died without finding a cent for all his labour.

Con had another side to his nature. When he learned that a neighbour was terribly ill, he went to his place and cut an enormous amount of firewood to see him through until he got well.

The Perrys have other memories of events that took place along the river that runs by their door. Such as the time a young Native lad decided to fall a cottonwood tree with which he intended to build a dugout canoe. He sawed the tree down and as soon as it hit the ground a mother black bear and two cubs tumbled out of it. The mother was killed by the crash, but the two cubs survived. The two cubs were sustained with dog food until a game warden picked them up and shipped them to a zoo.

Sometimes animals do the strangest things, such as the heifer Esther had to deal with while attempting to give it some shots. The animal broke through the wall of the lumber barn and ran away. It never returned.

There was also an interesting story about a horse they owned, which John described as a French Coach horse. When they changed to tractors from horses on the ranch, this horse was sold to a sawmill operator. For some unknown reason the horse went crazy in the barn and beat the blazes out of the other horses, then ran away into the forest. The entire mill crew was sent to search for the animal, but it was never found.

The Perrys had many confrontations with bears throughout the years. John recalled one hunt that had a surprise ending. A hunter from Willow River was following the river near their ranch when he came upon a grizzly with a moose leg in its mouth. He only had a 32-20 rifle with him, but he fired three shots and wounded the bear. Although it was seriously wounded, the bear made for the hunter and chased him away. The hunter came to the ranch and told the men his story, suggesting that they go after it with their bigger 30-30 rifles. John and Miles followed the bear a short distance through the snow and were greatly impressed by its huge tracks. Darkness was approaching, so the men quit tracking and went home. The next morning they took up the trail and followed a short distance when they came to a spot where the grizzly circled the evening before. It had waited beside the trail to ambush them. At some point the bear had tired of the wait and moved on. Both men realized that had they ventured 100 metres (328 feet) further the previous evening, they may well have been killed. Immediately they turned and went home where they informed the hunter that since he had wounded the bear, it was his duty to finish it off. The hunter refused so the destiny of the bear remains unknown.

On another hunt, Miles and John met a grizzly that was following the bank of the river. They stood behind a cottonwood tree hoping the bear would pass without sensing their presence. The bear appeared to be passing them when it suddenly turned and ran straight at them. Miles fired three shots and the bear tumbled down the bank into the river. John ran along the bank and kept pace with the drifting bear until it hit shallow water. Then the

Grizzly bear.

two men pulled it into shore and began studying it. At once they noticed something was terribly wrong with its jaw. An eight centimetre (three-inch) piece of jaw had been broken and was turned inside out with the teeth facing the flesh of the inner mouth. It had completely healed over, so it was obvious that the injury had occurred sometime earlier. The bear was all grey in colour, the only bear they ever found that way. It was in pathetic condition with its teeth mostly rotted away; this may well have been a factor in its attack on the men.

Another bear story was given to John by a man named Bill Store. Bill trapped near McBride, BC, in the late 1930s and was walking along the river when a grizzly met him right at the edge of the riverbank. Bill was carrying a 25-20 rifle which was totally inadequate for grizzlies, but at the last instant he fired his gun right under the bear's jaw and the bullet pierced its brain. Bill showed John the enormous hide and claws he had taken from the bear as well as two pails of fat he had rendered down. Both men realized that Bill's guardian angel must have been on duty that day. Bill moved into a cabin at the Perry Ranch and spent many summers prospecting the Willow River. When Bill reached retirement age and received his pension cheques, he acted like a millionaire. Perhaps it was the first time he received a steady income!

July 1936 turned out to have a shocking surprise for John. He was crossing one of his hay fields when he saw a moose running toward him. It threw him into the air and attempted to trample him several times. In between the attacks, he ran into a barn only to have the moose follow him. John realized that he would not survive unless he got away from the moose, so he managed to climb into a hayloft where the moose could not follow. For at least an hour the moose circled the barn and even bunted it several times before it left the area. Only when it was leaving did John see a calf that had been hiding by the barn.

During the attack John had stuck a double-bitted axe into the moose's head. Though he searched the area thoroughly, to this day he has never found that axe. Immediately after the attack John was taken to Prince George where he was examined by Dr. Lyons who found no serious damage. Only when John was X-rayed several years later was it found that he had endured three broken ribs.

During the Depression many immigrants took up homesteads

along the Willow River. One such homestead was across the river and about eight kilometres (five miles) upstream of the Perry Ranch. John recalls the day, when he was about sixteen years of age, when an exciting event took place. It was during the winter of 1935 when the Polish homesteader crossed the open river on a down-tree and made his way to their home. Exhausted from fighting his way through the snow, he told the Perrys that his wife was unable to deliver and in desperate need of help. John was elected to ride to Prince George for medical help, so he saddled a near-wild pony and attempted the thirty-kilometre (seventeen-mile) trip. What with fighting the wild bronco, which threw itself upside down at one point, it took him five hours to reach town. He proceeded to one of the three doctors in town, only to be told that he was too old to endure the trip. The second doctor came with the same response. John contacted the police and together they went to the other doctor, a younger man named Eric Dupries, who agreed to go if they could supply a ride. John went to a local garage and was told that a vehicle could be ready in two hours if they could find a driver. John was only sixteen and had no driver's license, so he was told to walk to the airport where a man lived who could do the driving. This entailed a ten-kilometre (six-mile) round trip walk, and when John returned with the driver, the owner wanted to know who would pay for the vehicle use. It was suggested that since the stricken people were on relief, there must be government assistance for such an emergency. Again, John had to walk to the government agent's home to get permission, which he achieved.

At last the doctor, along with a nurse in dress and high heels were headed out to the Giscome Turnoff, where Miles waited with horses and sleigh. By the time they arrived at the Perry Ranch, it was morning so they all sat down to a hearty breakfast. Miles told the doctor and nurse in frank words that she was not going to the homestead because it was going to be a tough trip. The doctor relented and they started out on the eight-kilometre (five-mile) trek through the forest. They arrived at Spey Creek to find it full of water and snow. Miles put his axe to work and built a bridge out of poles, then found that the horses refused to cross. Once again Miles showed his ingenuity by blindfolding the horses. This time they crossed. Three kilometres (two miles) further along they came to the Willow River, only to find part of the channel open.

Once more Miles cut poles and at last they got across to the home-stead. It was somewhat of a shock to find three young girls there with their ill mother. They had been living on moose meat that the Perrys had supplied for them and vegetables from a garden, without a school anywhere in the area—such were the hardships suffered by many of the pioneers.

A few hours later, the baby was successfully delivered and the party was on their way back to the ranch, where they arrived ut-terly exhausted and soaked to their waists. At that time, the doc-tor assured them that the mother would not have lasted another twelve hours. Now it was John's turn to take the doctor and nurse back to the highway where the driver and car were to be waiting. Without knowing why, John threw a toolbox into the sleigh; this turned out to be their salvation. A few kilometres before the high-way, they were astounded to find the car. The driver had got tired of waiting without any food, so he tried to drive in to the ranch. He was terribly stuck and another few hours were wasted getting the car back to solid ground. When the car was started, it became obvious that the clutch had been seriously damaged attempting to get unstuck. John crawled under and found the problem—he ad-justed the clutch and at last they were on their way back to Prince George.

About fifty years went by when two of the young Polish girls arrived at the Perry Ranch. They discussed the events from the long ago, and said that the baby boy not only survived, but that that he was doing well logging, on Vancouver Island.

John then added a footnote to the story of the baby/mother rescue by remembering a statement Miles had made when he re-turned with the doctor from the emergency trip, "The greatest thrill of my life was when we crossed the open river; I found myself praying that the ice and the poles would not let go."

The year 1953 turned out to be a nightmare for John. He was working on the conveyor at their sawmill when he was struck and fell six metres (twenty feet), landing on his back on the frozen ground. The back of his skull split open rendering him uncon-scious, a state he stayed in for several days. He was taken to Prince George and transferred to Vancouver General Hospital by aircraft the same day.

The prognosis was heartbreaking; Miles was informed that if

John survived he would be a vegetable. Three years passed during which time he underwent many operations. The cost was horrendous. John had an insurance policy that would have covered him, but as bad luck would have it, the company declared bankruptcy just three days before he was injured. John had ten thousand dollars in the bank, which was a considerable nest egg at that time. Not only did he use it all up, but he borrowed a great deal from others, which he had to repay later. One day a collection agency informed him that they were going after his share of the ranch. Realizing the nightmare that could arise from such action, John hired a lawyer. The lawyer's first order of business was to arrange a back-dated bill of sale of the property to Miles and Esther. The court action died a quick death.

John told me that there were fifty other men in the paraplegic ward with him. He also noted that many of them drank themselves to death in the ensuing years. After three years in Vancouver, John returned home—wheelchair bound for the rest of his life. How did he respond to his new life? Perhaps the best way to answer that is by relating my first meeting with him. Part of my work with the Protection Branch of the Ministry of Forests was to inspect fire permit applications to ascertain that the burn would be conducted in a safe manner. Such was my order of business the day I arrived at the Perry Ranch. As I got out of my truck, I heard a chainsaw running behind a nearby building, so I walked around to get a necessary signature for the permit. My first view of John was one I shall never forget. Here was a man strapped into a wheelchair so he couldn't fall out. In his hands he held a chainsaw and the blocks were falling fast and furious. My first thought was that someone should tell this man that he is seriously injured and cannot possibly run a chainsaw. The best was yet to come however, because when I returned from the inspection, John was splitting the blocks with an axe. He would stand the blocks on end with the axe and then strike them and, believe me, they came apart.

When he arrived home from his three-year ordeal, John promised himself that he would not be a burden on anyone. That winter he cut and split sixty cords of firewood which readily sold in Prince George.

John had several encounters with irate moose throughout the years and was treed on a few occasions. One interesting encounter

Author inspecting a communal porcupine den at 1,700-metre (5,577-feet) elevation.

occurred when he was in the process of cutting up a huge fir log for firewood. As soon as he started the chainsaw, he noticed a cow moose approaching. As he had previously been seriously beaten by a moose, he took no chances and ran his wheelchair to his Jeep. He just got himself and the dog loaded when the cow came right to the Jeep, so John wisely left the area. When he returned for a look, he found a calf moose lying right behind the fir log he had intended to cut up. Again, John left the area and returned two days later to find the moose had left.

John tells an interesting story about Mr. Blackburn who moved into the Blackburn area of Prince George when John was but a child. Apparently he had a large field sown with oats and, when it was only a month out of the ground, the moose found it. In an effort to save part of the crop, a group of people went to the area and attempted to scare the moose away. The effort failed in that it was the people that left the area on the run, instead of the moose. No doubt about it, moose and bears are simply crazy about oat fields. The big difference between the two is that bears not only eat the oats, they also roll around in the oat field and destroy much more than they eat. Worth noting, Mr. Blackburn was only one of several pioneers that were killed by their own bulls.

When I questioned John about losing cattle to predators, he informed me that during the early years on the ranch they only lost cattle and hogs to black bears, most of which they tracked down and shot. It was around the thirties when grizzlies and wolves started taking their toll. He surprised me by stating that they lost twenty calves to wolves last year. A conservation officer came out and attempted to trap them but he only managed to catch one calf and no wolves. One of their female employees—Debbie Hallam—managed to get six wolves and that took some of the pressure off.

Throughout the years the Perry Ranch has lost many cattle to bears and wolves, but I must admit that I was surprised to learn that they have lost more cattle over the last ten years than all the previous years combined. Most of the kills are caused by wolves. When bears are involved, the killing technique is always the same— a heavy slap to the neck resulting in a broken neck. The power in a bear's forearm is indeed formidable.

When I asked John about the numbers in wolf packs, he responded by telling me about a pack of fifty wolves that he ran into by the Bowron River during the winter of 1936. They were across the river from him at a distance of a few hundred metres so he aimed about half a metre (two feet) over their backs and bagged three. The river was partly open so he had to fall a tree across the open portion in order to get the pelts. That provided him with a cheque for seventy-five dollars in bounty money, which at that time was equal to a couple months' pay.

I wondered if the large number of wolves in the pack was due to early spring mating rituals, but John was not certain. The reason I asked was because I had several old-time trappers tell me that they had found where two packs had merged on a lake or river during February. Possibly it was just curiosity that made them check each other out during mating season. John also concurs that something major has taken place with wolf packs in the last sixty years. Whereas it used to be a common event to see packs with thirty or more wolves, one seldom sees more than ten in a pack anymore.

I was interested in John's interactions with wolves. He told me that many times the wolves came and peed on their chainsaws and gas cans. Sometimes they would do this while the men were gone for lunch. This shows that the wolves were close by, although the men never got a glimpse of them. It seems obvious that the wolves were letting the men know that this was their territory.

Yet another wolf story took place the day John took his rifle and walked upriver to try for a deer. Suddenly a deer swam across and climbed the bank right in front of him. The deer was exhausted so John knew it was being chased. A minute later a wolf with six pups swam across the river, hot on the deer's trail. John shot a couple of them and the others retreated back across the river. John had two dogs with him and they immediately crossed the river and then all hell broke loose, such as a lot of yelping and racket he had never heard before. Suspecting that the dogs were being torn apart, John waded the river and came upon the animals, but they were not locked in mortal combat; there was a lot more noise than action. The adult wolf had been wounded, so when John approached, she lunged at him. John tried to fire his rifle only to find he had a dud in the barrel. He struck the wolf over the head and then fired another shot that ended the battle. When the dust cleared, John had four wolves and one hundred dollars in bounty money. Puzzled by the dud cartridge, John tested the other cartridges in the box and found eight out of twenty were duds.

This story reminded me of a story told by my father. When he trapped back in the thirties, he ran into a box of bullets that were almost useless. One of the 285-grain bullets from his 38-55 had barely penetrated the hide of a moose. Obviously these cartridges were contaminated in some manner.

Proof of one of John's wolf stories still rests in the ranch house in the form of an exceptionally large wolf. This wolf used to swim the river and harass the cattle that were penned up some distance from the ranch house. Sometimes after these attacks it took hours to round up the cattle and get them back into the pen. One day John managed to get a shot at the head of the pack and he got it. The strange part of this tale is that for two weeks after he shot this wolf a large pack of wolves gathered on a hill across the river and howled for hours every night. Surely this wolf must have been their leader.

John told me that one of the biggest surprises during his many years on the ranch is the appearance of large herds of elk. They were unknown in the area until about ten years ago. Now they have seen herds of up to forty animals. Most certainly the logging is responsible for their increase, as it provides an endless amount of feed. When I asked John if the elk herds were in conflict with their cattle for range, he replied, "No, there is an abundance of feed to go around."

It seems that there is always something to cause excitement around their ranch, such as the night Esther awoke to her dog making strange sounds outside their door. She rushed out to find a cougar on top of her dog, viciously chewing its neck to pieces. She got a rifle and fired point-blank into the cat, which jumped over a pile of lumber and disappeared into the night. Esther immediately

Grizzlies like to follow streams.

phoned their employee Debbie, and together they started making circles in the snow, searching for the cat. When they completed the circle they knew the cat was still close by, so they awaited daylight. At first light, they followed the blood trail and found the dead cat only fifteen metres (forty-nine feet) from the house. That one bullet had taken care of the cat, and a two hundred dollar vet bill took care of the dog.

That same day they found that the cougar had been denned up in one of their sheds. Not exactly a warm feeling to know they had been under the cat's watchful eyes for some time.

Just this past summer Esther had another confrontation with a cougar. She was baling hay with a tractor when two young deer ran right to her. Instantly she knew something had to be chasing them so she glanced around to find a cougar hot on their trail. The two deer jumped a fence and swam the Willow River. For some strange reason the cougar did not jump the fence, instead it followed along looking for a place to get through it. Esther gave chase with the tractor and the cougar fled in the same direction it came from. By that time the deer were long gone.

John related another story about cougars when he told me that many years ago a Native trapper got several of them around the Willow Canyon. When I suggested there must have been game trails in that area that kept the cougars hanging around, he assured me that there were game trails criss-crossing each other around the canyon area.

The Perrys had yet another episode with cougars. They moved five late-arrival calves out to their Giscome farm to protect them from the larger stock that kept them from feeding. The man who was tending the calves notified them that the calves had all been killed. Upon arriving at the farm, they found fresh tracks of a female cougar and two kittens. They had only devoured a tiny amount of flesh. The traps were reset but the cougars never returned.

Another exciting experience occurred the day John went to check on their cattle in the Jeep that has hand controls for his use. As he patrolled the pasture, he came upon a big red cow that had been freshly killed. A large pile of earth had been built into a cone shape and the cow had been carried, not dragged, and placed on top of the cone of earth. Brother Miles came to the site and skinned out the neck of the cow so they could determine the cause of death. A broken neck was the answer and the obvious conclusion was that it had been killed by a bear. Later that day John was hiding nearby when a grizzly came out to feed; four well-placed shots took care of the bear. The next day when Fish and Wildlife personnel examined the bear they stated, "What were you trying to do, make hamburger?"

Something I did not realize until I had wandered the mountains for many years is that porcupines have large dens high in the mountains where they bunch up during the winter. I have seen a small cave about five metres square (fifty-four square feet) with fifteen centimetres (six inches) of feces spread across the floor and a considerable amount pushed outside. One can but guess just how many porcupines it took over the years to accumulate all those feces. On two occasions I went to these dens in winter only to find the den was covered with four and a half metres (fifteen feet) of snow-drift. I didn't have the energy to dig them out.

Porcupines have always caused a great deal of grief to the Perrys. Throughout the years they have had a variety of different barns on their properties to avoid having to move the horses for long distances. A constant worry was that the porcupines would get into the mangers, and once the horses put their heads down to eat, they would get a slap across the nose. This resulted in a tough job of removing the quills because the horses would fight them. A pair of scissors was used to cut the ends off the quills which were then more easily removed with pliers.

Some of their dogs were even more of a problem in that they did not seem to learn. Often after the painful procedure of removing the quills, the dogs would go back the next day and return home with another face full of quills. I was rather surprised to learn that the porcupines would sometimes den-up in their hay barns and stink up the hay to the point where the horses refused to eat it. Cows are often rather curious animals, so it is no surprise to learn that they would approach the porcupines to check them out and receive a face full of quills in return.

John recalled the summer evening they were sitting on their porch when a skunk came along and walked right between their two dogs that were stretched out resting. At once the two dogs grabbed the skunk by each end and proceeded to tear it apart. The result was a porch that stunk horribly for many months. Every time it rained and the dogs got wet, the stink would return. Perhaps it is understandable if the dogs lacked attention for quite some time after that debacle.

About four years ago, Debbie, a ranch employee, took a rifle and went with a truck to check a fence line. She left the rifle in the truck and when she returned, she found a skunk spraying each of the tires on the vehicle. The stench was so bad that she backed off for a while. Finally she got the nerve to get the rifle and dispatch the critter. Again, the stink stayed with the vehicle for many months.

Three years ago, Esther was following the river about five kilometres (three miles) from the ranch when she stumbled onto a crippled horse. It was feeding on their range and drinking from a small stream. When the stream dried up and the horse needed water, it jumped down about (six metres) twenty feet to the river's edge and this may have been where it acquired the hip injury. Since there was no feed available to the horse, it had to be moved or it would face starvation. Esther brought her pick-up truck with side-rails to the spot and dug a trench down to the river; with a great deal of effort they managed to get the horse aboard and brought it to the ranch. An ad was placed in the newspaper to the effect that the horse had been legally quarantined and one hundred dollars would release it to the owner. One day a man arrived and claimed it was his horse but he refused to pay the money. Instead he maintained that the SPCA had given him permission to take the horse. A phone call to the SPCA quickly dispelled that nonsense and so Esther locked the horse in a corral. When the man threatened to tear down the gate, Esther made the pretense of phoning the police. The threat worked, and the gentleman left the horse in their care. Did the horse get well, you ask? No, instead it has been a freeloader on the Perry Ranch for the last three years.

For many years Roy Spurr owned Eagle Lake Sawmills at Giscome, which was an eleven-kilometre (seven-mile) haul on a winter road from the Perry Ranch. A great deal of their beef and hay, along with twenty tons of potatoes, was sold on an annual basis to the mill. One of the reasons Mr. Spurr bought from them was because he had been taken to the cleaners when dealing with others. In one instance he bought a carload of hay from the prairies only to find that it contained almost all rose bushes. In another deal he purchased several hundred-pound bags of potatoes only to find rocks in the centre of the bags.

Near the end of our interviews, I asked John to sum up his life. Without a second's hesitation he replied, "If I had it to do over, I would do it exactly the same except for one thing—I would be a little more careful."

The oldest brother, Miles, passed away last year at the age of ninety-two. John now resides in a hospital in Prince George, while the ranch has been left in the capable hands of Esther and her employees.

During the last twenty years I have spent many hours listening to John's adventurous life stories, and although all were interesting, without a doubt my favourite is the following:

This story began back in the forties during late November when two prospectors working the river told Miles and John that they had shot a big bull moose near the Willow Canyon. They had taken most of the meat, but had left a magnificent set of antlers at the site because they were fully loaded carrying the meat and their supplies. The two brothers grabbed their 30-30 rifles, got on their saddle horses and headed for the canyon to retrieve the antlers. A short distance from the moose carcass, they tied the horses, then continued on foot through a thicket of young spruce forest. As they approached the remains, a large grizzly bear exploded through the thicket toward them, slapping the thick, young trees out of its way as it approached. Both men began working their rifles and a volley of shots echoed through the forest. The bear finally succumbed and settled to the ground less than five metres from where they were standing.

They skinned out the bear, except for the head, rolled it up in a ball and managed to pack it back to where the horses were tied. Several times they tried to lift this package, which they guessed to be about 125 kilograms (275 pounds), onto one of the horses, but were unable to do so because of the weight. Searching for a way out of their dilemma, they took the horse into a gulley, placed some poles on the horse's back and at last got the bear hide and head loaded. The men then returned to the bear and began stripping the abundant fat off its body. At last they were fully loaded and homeward bound.

While Mile's wife rendered down the fat, which produced 70

kilograms (150 pounds) of lard, the men returned to the bear and retrieved the twelve bullets from the carcass. They also counted out the number of cartridges that had been fired and it came to twelve. None had missed their intended target. Both men were impressed to the point that they still have the twelve bullets in a jar. When I asked if the men were a bit excited during the bear's attack, John replied, "When the gunfire quieted down Miles and I looked at each other and noticed that we were both sweating profusely." John then shook his head for emphasis and added, "That was a day to remember."

CONSPIRACY
OF SILENCE

Shortly after the completion of the Grand Trunk Pacific Railway through central British Columbia in 1914, a great number of trappers moved into the surrounding forests. As the registration of traplines on Crown land did not come into effect until 1926, it was a case of first come, first served. Often this meant that two trappers would find that they both wanted the same piece of forest. This can and did lead to trouble—such as was suspected after the disappearance of William Allen Goodson along what was known as the Raging River and the Clearwater River. These streams are now known as the Torpy River and Walker Creek. Both streams drain into the Fraser River a few miles northeast of Dome Creek, which is situated about 140 kilometres (87 miles) east of Prince George, BC.

In my first book *Crazy Man's Creek*, published in 1998, I told the story of Goodson's disappearance after a fight with trapper Emmet Baxter "Shorty" Haines, which occurred during the winter of 1925–26. But I think it best to start this story back in 1909 when Haynes first arrived in this area. The story was carried in the Fort George *Tribune* dated November 13, 1909:

BEAR RIVER TRAPPER REPORTED DROWNED

Late last spring Jack Dawson and E.B. Haynes left Barkerville intending to go north to the Fox River, a tributary of the Findlay River to engage in trapping.

They crossed to Bear Lake and went down the Bear, now known as the Bowron River. En route they met parties from the north who told them that two outfits were then on the Fox River and others intended to go there. This information made them change their plans, and they decided to return to Bear River to trap on it this winter. They returned and established camps, their upper camp being at a point about fifty-six kilometres (thirty-five miles) above the mouth of the river. Of late they have been making preparations to cut trails on which to set a line of traps. On Saturday morning November 6th, Dawson left the cabin to go downstream to engage at the work, while Haynes went upstream. They had a canoe a mile below the cabin, and Dawson was to take it and go on down to where they had a tent and a boat, some seven or eight miles, where they intended to build a winter covering for the boat and canoe. On returning to the cabin on Saturday evening, Haynes did not find Dawson there, as he expected; a dog that had gone with him was there. He fired several shots, but got no answer. He went down to where the canoe had been tied; but there were no signs there. It was then too late to make further search and he returned to the cabin. Early Sunday morning Haynes resumed the search. He went down the river to the tent and boat, but saw no trace of Dawson or the canoe. He came to the conclusion that Dawson was drowned, the river being obstructed in places by log-jams and sweepers, which are dangerous if care is not exercised in passing them. Haynes searched down the river to the Fraser and came on to Fort George, where he arrived on Tuesday night. He reported the facts to James Cowie, manager of the Hudson's Bay Company store, who is a justice of the peace. On Thursday morning, Haynes, accompanied by Bob Alexander and Frank Seymour, started over the trail for Bear River, a three-day trip. Dawson lived at Van Winkle seven years, was an Englishman, and forty-three years of age.

The Bear (Bowron) River was frozen over when the men arrived so the search was aborted. On November 27, 1909 the *Tribune* added:

Bob Alexander and Frank Seymour returned on Tuesday from Bear River, where they went with E.B. Haynes, whose partner, Jack Dawson, disappeared on November 10th, and was supposed to have been drowned in the river. When the party reached Bear River it was froze over, and there was no chance to make a search for the missing man, so Alexander and Seymour returned, making the return trip in three days. They passed traps set out by Mary, an aged Indian woman who was a belle in Barkerville fifty years ago. Though no longer a belle, she is considered one of the best hunters in the village and cares for a number of orphan children. She is seldom broke, and when she is, she makes a call at the Hudson's Bay Company store and makes her wants known. She seldom goes away empty-handed.

Picture of William Goodson at his cabin at The Forks, c 1925.
COURTESY THE EXPLORATION PLACE P986.38.53

A Dog Team on the Fraser River at Fort George, B. C.   No. 105.

"Shorty" hauling mail up the Fraser River, 1910.

I found nothing to indicate that there was anything suspicious about Dawson's disappearance. Obviously it was considered an accident. After all these years have passed there is no way to know if there had been harsh words between Haynes and Dawson before he went under the logjam. Perhaps I am out of line to even consider such a thing.

Shorty quickly built up a solid reputation in the Fort George District by delivering mail over 200 kilometres (124 miles) up the frozen Fraser River during the years 1910–12. This mail was desperately needed by the engineers and surveyors along the G.T.P. Railway grade.

Another claim to fame occurred when Shorty and a man named Wood started a business transporting boats and supplies through the Giscome Portage to Summit Lake. They were in direct competition with Seabach and Huble of Giscome Portage fame and they were in business for less than a year before they gave up the venture.

Shorty spent several years trapping the Pass Lake and Upper Torpy River area, which was where he was situated when he got into the brutal fight with Goodson. After Goodson disappeared, rumours floated throughout the North, often connecting Shorty Haynes to his disappearance. I questioned many people in the Dome Creek area regarding their feud, but the first tangible information came to me from Chris Gleason, who also trapped the adjacent McGregor River area from 1915–24. Chris was living in Dome Creek when this incident occurred. In 1976, I visited Chris in White Rock, BC, and asked him if he knew anything about Goodson's disappearance. Chris replied that he had known about it all through the years and then added, "All the others are dead now, so I may as well tell you fellows or else it will die with me, "Shorty and Goodson had trouble going back to the war [World War One] and things didn't get any better. Finally, they got into a terrible fight in 1925 and when it was over, Goodson was carried from a house party to a riverboat in an unconscious state."

Chris further stated that Shorty had done away with Goodson because after their fight, Goodson had burned one of his cabins, including a winter supply of food. When I asked about the story that Shorty had been a Texas Ranger during his youth Chris added, "He never told me that, but I knew that he was a dead shot with both rifle and handgun." When I questioned Chris about Goodson stating that Shorty had struck him with a hammer during their fight, he replied, "If you seen the size of Shorty's fist, you would believe it felt like a hammer." Chris then left me with the distinct impression that Shorty simply did what had to be done.

Perhaps a hint of what kind of man Goodson had tangled with can be derived from this brief note in the Prince George *Citizen* on July 23, 1919:

Shorty Haynes arrived back from France and Germany Saturday night. He enlisted with the 102nd and served two years on sniper duty during the war. One of the first white men in this section [1909], Shorty is sure glad to be back in God's country, and says he has seen enough of Europe to last him for the rest of his days. The reverse English applies to the cognomen of Shorty, as he stands something over six feet and is the type of soldier that made Canada famous.

When I pursued the burnt cabin story in the Dome Creek area, several other trappers from the area told me that they were certain that there had been no cabin burning, although they were elusive about or unaware of the cause of the Haynes/Goodson bitter feud.

About 1940 Shorty gave up trapping the Torpy River area and moved to Decker Lake, BC, where he went into retirement. His neighbours at Decker Lake were a family named Paulson, whose lives became entwined with Shorty's.

Perhaps a year after my book *Crazy Man's Creek* was published I met Paul Paulson, who grew up living next door to Shorty at Decker Lake. Paul states that during the 1930s and '40s, he learned a great deal from this knowledgeable woodsman and added that he was at Shorty's bedside shortly before he passed away in 1953.

Paul was just a young lad when his father drowned in Decker Lake. As a result his mother took in washing and did odd jobs, thereby managing to raise the family on her own. One of Paul's stories concerned Shorty's love for homebrew and the effect it had on his family. Apparently Shorty made some brew and then threw the mash outdoors where the Paulson milk cow found it. The cow cleaned it all up and died shortly after. A few days later the Paulsons arose to find a milk cow tied up at their door. Although Shorty never admitted to his involvement, they were certain that he was the donor.

Paul Paulson with elk taken at Kluachesi Lake.

Shorty was always admired for the quality of moonshine he produced, and the police were well aware of this talent. Paul tells about the time the police were sneaking along Decker Lake

Emmet Shorty Haines and Carl Swanson at Goodson's cabin, c 1930.

toward Shorty's cabin when they were spotted. Acting quickly, Shorty threw a bag of salt into the mixture just as the police rushed in the cabin door. The brew was seized and sent away for identification. When the case was pursued in court, the judge was notified that whatever it was, it was not fit for human consumption. Once again, Shorty remained a free man.

Paul tells how Shorty built a steam bath and a diving board on the lake and then taught the youngsters how to dive and swim. Paul also learned to trap from this master of the trapline. Paul also told the story about the day a man named Alf Noon paid a visit to Shorty. They got into the moonshine and once Alf got hammered, his reputed sarcasm came to the fore. Shorty made him some bacon and eggs and was repaid by Alf telling him that it was just fit for dogs. A neighbour woman heard loud voices emanating from the cabin, and then Alf came out the door with Shorty hot on his tail, brandishing a weapon in his hand. Alf had short legs but he got them moving and made his escape by boat, with Shorty breathing down his neck.

This was just some of many stories Paul has to tell about this noted woodsman, and he makes no effort to hide his admiration for the man.

Sgt. W. Walker and the Estonian Count. The Sergeant admitted it was a strange case.
THE VALLEY MUSEUM AND ARCHIVE 2003.26.233

When I showed Paul the evidence I had in my possession concerning the Haynes/Goodson feud, he filled me in on a story that had been told to him by Carl Swanson, one of Shorty's friends at Decker Lake.

Carl told Paul that he, too, had trapped the Dome Creek area at the time of William Goodson's disappearance; he further added that he had attended a trappers' meeting in Dome Creek during early winter 1925–26 where the topic of discussion was what they should do about a fur thief in the area. Shorty made it clear to all at the meeting that he would deal with the problem, and just a short time later Goodson went missing.

A thorough police investigation followed the report that Goodson had disappeared, as attested to by this article in the Prince George *Citizen* dated March 11, 1926:

POLICE SEARCH FOR MISSING DOME CREEK TRAPPER

Sergeant Walker, of the Provincial Police, has instituted a search for William Allan Goodson, a trapper who has made Dome Creek his headquarters for a number of years. The initial move in the search was entrusted to Constable Sam Service, of McBride. Upon a visit to Dome Creek he ascertained that Goodson made a trip out from his trapline to Dome Creek on October 14th for the purchase of supplies. Goodson at this time left a letter with James Stewart, postmaster, with instructions that he turn the same over to the police upon the next visit to Dome Creek of any member of the force. There was no police visit and Stewart was holding the letter when Goodson returned on November 2nd for further supplies. He made enquiries about the letter he had left with Stewart and asked for its return. It happened the letter had been misplaced and Stewart was unable to return it. Goodson got the supplies he wanted and headed back for his trapline, situated at the junction of the Torpy and Clearwater Rivers, about nineteen kilometres (twelve miles) from McBride. [Actually eighty kilometres (fifty miles) from McBride.]

So far as Stewart could remember Goodson appeared to be in good health. His visit to Dome Creek is the last record of his having been seen. On February 26th, in company with E.B. Haines and another resident, Constable Service started on a trip to the Goodson cabin, which was reached next day. It was found to be in good condition, and there was no evidence of a struggle. The dishes had been washed and put away. There was no fur in the cabin, neither was there any tobacco, and the inference was that Goodson had left the cabin to secure further supplies.

Among the papers found in the cabin was a voluminous writing in the nature of a journal, which was commenced on October 4th and continued with a few breaks down to November 12th. The subject matter related to a fight which Goodson said he had with E.B. Haines, in the course of which he alleged he had been hit with a hammer. From his writings one would gather that for a time he feared his injuries would prove fatal, but he appeared to be going strong when he visited Dome Creek on November 2nd, although upon his return to the cabin he resumed his writing and kept it going until November 12th.

So much snow had fallen that it was impossible for Constable Service to track Goodson from his cabin. In cruising around in the bush before reaching the cabin the constable and E.B. Haines had come upon a rifle suspended in a tree, which Haynes said belonged to Goodson. The circumstance that Goodson was known to carry a pistol while in the bush was offered as an explanation for his leaving the rifle in a tree.

E.B. Haines is said to admit having a quarrel with Goodson some time ago, but contends it did not amount to anything, and he denies that a hammer or any other kind of weapon was used. The police enquiry is to be carried further with a view to locating Goodson. He carried a substantial balance in one of the Prince George banks and made no withdrawals from his account since September last.

The missing man was well-known in McBride and vicinity. He was fifty-eight-years-old, stood six feet two inches and weighed 86 kilograms (190 pounds). He saw service in the world war and up until August last was in receipt of a monthly pension of fifteen dollars on account of injuries received. This pension was cut off after August, following a medical examination, when Goodson's condition was found to be normal. From letters found in his cabin, Goodson is believed to have a wife, Mrs. Mabel Goodson, of Columbus, Ohio, and a son, L.W. Goodson, of Newark, Ohio.

Several months had passed since Goodson was last seen; this meant that all sign had long since vanished. The fact that Shorty was allowed to lead the police search appears to be beyond comprehension; however, since it appears that many people were involved in the cover-up, perhaps there was not a better choice available. As well, the rifle taken by police as evidence was not Goodson's rifle.

"Shorty" along the Torpy River, c 1935. Goodson's cabin in background.
COURTESY JIM CHAMBERS.

I have recently learned that a young trapper from an adjacent trapline had found a rifle in the tree and since it was a new 30-30, he took it and left his old 30-30 in its place.

I was greatly surprised that the police appeared to place little interest in the fact that all of Goodson's furs had disappeared. This holds great significance, because just three years ago a man named Mickey McMillan offered an interesting addition to the Goodson story. He told me that he had been born in Bend, just five kilometres (three miles) from Dome Creek. He claimed that his mother

Shorty Haynes and trapper/guide Jim Hooker with grizzly bear, c 1920.
COURTESY JIM CHAMBERS.

told him that she had a visitor about the same time that Goodson disappeared; a neighbouring trapper who was a close friend to Shorty. This man asked his mother if he could store a supply of furs in her hay barn for a time. The trapper was extremely nervous, but offered no explanation for his actions.

The missing furs, the missing letter, so many factors that seem to indicate a great number of people were at least knowledgeable of Goodson's fate.

After several frustrating and fruitless searches, this article appeared in the *Citizen* on May 13, 1926:

> Provincial Constables Service and Martin returned on Sunday evening following a fruitless search for W.A. Goodson, the trapper who disappeared from his cabin seventeen miles up the Fraser River from Dome Creek during the latter part of February. The disappearance of Goodson is one of the most remarkable which the local police have been called upon to deal with.

For a time I wondered why Chris Gleason had told me the burnt cabin story, until I finally realized that he was attempting to protect the other families involved in the trappers' meeting. Since Chris knew that Shorty was the guilty party, he thought it best to let him take all the blame.

For several years I have known that Shorty left his trapline at Pass Lake shortly after Goodson's disappearance and took up residence on what had been Goodson's trapline. Just recently I found a picture of Goodson at his cabin on the forks of the Torpy River and Walker Creek. I also have a picture of Shorty and Carl Swanson at Goodson's cabin taken just a few years later. In short, it seems obvious that Shorty not only did away with Goodson, he immediately left his trapline in the Pass Lake area and took over Goodson's trapline and cabins as well.

Constable Sam Service was an intelligent and experienced police officer. This begs the question as to why he let the chief suspect in Goodson's disappearance lead the search party. I suggest that he did this deliberately in an attempt to trick Shorty or have him slip up in some way. If that was his intent, it appears obvious that the plan failed.

Was there any justice in this entire episode? When I question this, my mind always returns to a statement made by Chris Gleason when I last saw him, "I knew Shorty for a long time, and he was a good man and a just man."

One thing that appears certain is just how much Shorty impressed area trappers. This was clearly displayed when he suffered an accident, which was carried in the Prince George *Citizen* dated August 2, 1928:

> Shorty Haynes was brought in on Tuesday night's train to receive medical treatment for a badly shattered leg. Haynes met with his accident while riding a horse along the Clearwater trail in the Dome Creek section. The horse stumbled and threw Haynes against a stump, and then fell upon him. Haynes managed to crawl back to his cabin and when assistance arrived was brought into this city.

Jack Carnasky, a retired trapper in Dome Creek, told me that people rushed to Shorty's cabin when they learned he was injured. When I questioned Jack about what sort of man Goodson had been, he was extremely evasive. His only comment was, "Goodson was a smart aleck."

And so, because Shorty was so well admired and respected, many of his acquaintances refused and still refuse to accept the fact that he committed such a crime, or perhaps they secretly accept it and feel, as Chris Gleason did, that Goodson had it coming.

Some of Chris Gleason's words really hit home to me, such as his statement, "Shorty was the kind of fellow who boiled up slow, but when he did, he boiled up mighty hot." Whatever else may have happened, perhaps the real start of their feud lay in the first statement made by Chris Gleason, "They had trouble going back to the war." Since it is easy to imagine something serious happening on the battlefield, this could have been where the seeds for the feud originated. Another point worth noting is that the registration of traplines on Crown land started in 1926; this means that Shorty was the first registered owner of

Trapper Jack Carnasky with Old Samson, c 1919.
COURTESY CHRIS GLEASON.

Lawrence Hooker's son and Mickey McMillan.
PHOTO JACK BOUDREAU.

the Goodson's trapline.

After all these years have passed there is no way to know if Goodson was a fur thief, but if he was, then he surely had adopted a dangerous lifestyle; for there was no more certain way to die young than to be caught stealing furs in those days. One elderly trapper from Dome Creek put it rather succinctly when I asked him what he made of the entire Goodson mystery. After sitting in subdued silence for several minutes he responded with, "Whatever else happened, Goodson broke the code of the trail; it's as simple as that!"

Emmet Baxter Haynes passed away in the Burns Lake Hospital on January 30, 1953 at the age of seventy-five. One of his last visitors was his long-time friend Paul Paulson, who, like so many others, always thought the world of Shorty.

In the final analysis I think that the most surprising part of all was that their conspiracy of silence had held for over fifty years until all involved were dead. As with Dawson, Goodson's body was never found; the wilderness often keeps its secrets.

FIVE MEN
ON A RAFT

During the summer of 1929, a man named Helbak Kristensen and four other adventurers took a thirty-kilometre (nineteen-mile) walk through the mountains from Sinclair Mills in central BC to the Torpy River. Often referred to as the Clearwater River in the early-day local media, it was in fact known as the Raging River. The Clearwater River comprised just the eastern branch of the river, or what is now referred to as Walker Creek.

Three of the men—Helbakk, Axel and Aage Christensen were recent arrivals from Denmark—while Hilding and Hurtig Anderson hailed from Sweden.

Between July 1 and July 7, 1929, these men risked their lives rafting what to them was an unknown river. The intended three-day trip turned out to be a seven-day trip filled with danger, hunger and the intervention of the police when the overdue men were feared to have perished.

After the pictures of the trip were developed, Helbak sent them to Denmark along with the story that he had written on twenty-four postcards. Over the years the postcards sat in a box of pictures until some family members from Prince George went to Denmark for a visit. One of their cousins, Per Thomassen, told them about the postcards and offered to translate them into English. Two years ago, after sitting in Denmark for seventy-eight years, the story and pictures arrived in Prince George.

Helbak's translated story begins:

Day One:

I will try to tell the story of the trip which began because the sawmill we worked for closed for a three-day holiday. All five of us men decided we would use this holiday to climb over the mountains to the Clearwater River where we would build rafts and float down to the Fraser River and then back to Sinclair Mills again. We were equipped with guns, camera, an axe, food, tobacco and matches. We also carried nails and rope to build rafts.

We started July 1st at 4:00 a.m with heavy rucksacks and walked through the forest for seven kilometres following a game trail. We had to rest every half hour because of our heavy packs. After three hours we reached the mountain and that's where the hard work began; sometimes we had to crawl on our hands and knees. We shot a blue grouse on the mountain and took it along to cook later. We found out just how hard it was to climb with heavy packs, but we continued up the

Ready for the trip.

Climbing the mountain.

mountain. Gradually we climbed up to a clearing where we could see Sinclair Mills and the Fraser River behind us. The beautiful scenery cheered us up, and in a couple of hours we reached the mountaintop. Hurtig was unable to keep up with the others so I stayed behind with him. We arrived at the top about half an hour after the others and learned that they had seen four caribou. It was almost noon when we got to the top, so we rested for two hours before we started again.

What we did not know was that there was another mountain in our path, so we climbed it heading toward the east. We saw a moose this afternoon as well as some grizzly bear tracks. We took some wonderful pictures and at 7:00 p.m. we made camp one hundred metres from the summit. We made a fire and a bed of spruce boughs, then boiled water for tea and made dinner. After dinner we sat around the fire and discussed our trip until it was time to hit the blankets and get some sleep. We took turns standing guard and keeping the fire going all through the night.

The gang on the first ridge-top.

Day Two:

We got up at 5:00 a.m and washed in the little stream that ran by our camp, ate breakfast and continued across the mountain heading east. The mountain kept getting higher as we moved to the east. It was a sunny day and we were all in a good mood, singing songs. The land to the west is all covered with trees, but to the north and east are the big mountains that separate BC from Alberta [the Rocky Mountains]. We have seen many wolf tracks but have not seen the animals themselves.

After climbing and moving east for four hours we got past the mountain and could see down into the valley where the Clearwater River runs, but the forest was so thick we could not see the water. We started down the steep mountain and found that it is not any easier than climbing. We had to be careful not to fall. In some places we found snow and we slid down those slopes about a hundred metres with great speed. We were cold and wet, but we gained a lot of time by sliding. We stopped and ate lunch near the valley floor and from that point we could see the river for the first time. It was heavy forest, and as we followed the creek we came to a big canyon over a hundred metres deep.

We made our way around the canyon and by the time we reached the valley floor, Hurtig had lagged behind again because he was played out, so we had to carry part of his pack. We stopped for a piece of bread and spent some time looking for gold in the creek, but found nothing.

We rested for a while and walked only a hundred metres through the forest where we hit the river. The river was running fast and I guessed it to be a little bigger than the Gudenoen, Denmark's biggest river. The plan was to build two rafts, one two-man and one three-man and then let the two-man raft to go first so they could signal us if they found any falls or rapids in the river.

When it started to rain, we stopped and built a shelter to protect us from the rain. At the same time we started dragging parts of dry trees to the riverbank for raft construction, making certain that we took dry trees

Hilding on the mountaintop.

because they are lighter and float higher than green trees. At 8:00 p.m. we finished the rafts so we stretched out by the campfire. There was no guard put on duty this night because we were too tired.

Day Three:

We had a good night's sleep and at 6:00 a.m we started along the river with the rafts. All of our equipment was secured in the centre of the rafts, and we each had a long pole for controlling the rafts. Hilding and I went first so we could warn the others of logjams or falls. We went with great speed down the current, which was very strong and shortly the difficulties started. The raft

Snow sliding down toward the river.

shot around a tight bend in the river where it hit something and went under the water. Hilding managed to jump to shore, while I hung onto some trees to stop the raft from getting away from us until Hilding tied it up. We couldn't see the others, so we went back looking for them. We found them on the other side of the river—their raft went under a tree [sweep] that stuck out into the river. They had all been pushed off the raft into the water by the sweep. The raft was found down the river where it stuck fast in a logjam; luckily all the equipment was saved.

After that episode I rode alone on the raft while Hilding followed the shore to warn me of other obstacles in the water. The going along the bank was too tough for Hilding, so we added another log on the raft and he got back on. The big raft was ahead of us somewhere until we came around a bend and there was Axel standing on an island in the middle of the river, waving his arms and shouting that we had to get clear of their raft, but it was too late. We ran into their raft and our raft tipped up on its side, while we both jumped to the other side to keep it on an even keel. Axel told us that their raft had turned upside down and they had been under the water for a while. Hurtig and Aage were on the other side of the river where they had tied the raft. We tried to work the raft loose from the logjam, but the current was too strong and the rope hurt our hands. When we could not hold the raft any longer, Axel jumped aboard and rode it downriver until he got it tied up.

Hilding and I had to cross the river in order to join Hurtig and Aage, so we held hands and waded about halfway, where there was a small island that we managed to cross on. At that time we made a campfire and dried out all our blankets and clothes. We stood in our underwear around the fire until we were dry. Hilding and I were only wet to the waist, but the others had been underwater for quite a while.

This happened shortly before noon, so we held a

meeting to discuss our next course of action. We all agreed that it was too dangerous to continue rafting, so our options were to walk back over the mountains or follow the shore for sixty miles to the Fraser River, which we guessed would take three or four days. We were almost out of food, so we settled for the option of following the river because we knew that we could build another raft if the water tamed a bit. We also had the possibility of finding a trapper's cabin with some spare food.

Hilding and Aage took all the nails out of our rafts so we could build a new one; I spent some time taking about twenty pictures of the river. If you look close at the picture you can see the two men tearing the raft apart. Our lunch was just a piece of bread; we are into rations now.

We continued along the river as a rain fell and got

Building the raft.

us all wet. When we made camp Hurtig walked along the river to look for an animal for food, while I went the other direction, but we didn't find any animals. Hurtig shot at a goose and missed.

Day Four:

The next morning we found fresh moose tracks where one skirted our camp and carried on down the river. We followed the moose and found a game trail along the river. We tried to follow it but it disappeared in places where it was swampy. We had to jump from tuft to tuft at times, although the river appeared quite calm at this point.

Later that day we spotted two geese with goslings— they were swimming down the river. Axel and Hurtig both shot at them and one of the geese got hit, then it climbed the bank on the other side of the river and

Ready to sail.

went into the woods. Hilding and I decided to try to get the goose, as we needed food in the worst way. We followed the river until we found a spot where it was shallow enough for us to wade across, and then we stripped and waded out into the river where we found the water unbearably cold; it was coming down from the snow-covered mountains. The water was up to our waists, but with some difficulty we managed to find the goose and brought it back across the river where we rejoined the others. This was a big bird, probably about five kilograms. We made camp at noon, and then ate slices of the goose cooked in the frying pan. We had not eaten anything all day so it sure tasted good.

After we fed on the goose, we started building the new raft. It was difficult to find solid dry tree trunks. Most of the trees we fell just broke apart when they hit the ground, [the men were using western red cedar trees which are hollow and rotten] but we gathered five logs and then at last we found a big log to use and our raft was finished and ready for travel. While we worked on the raft, Hurtig walked back to camp to start supper and prepare the beds; he was not feeling good so we allowed him to do only light work.

We were all tired and hungry when we walked back to camp for supper, but we arrived to find Hurtig sound asleep. He had managed to fry the rest of the goose, but it was obvious that he was not well, because he offered Axel his ration of food if he would stand guard duty for him. I was immediately suspicious that he had already eaten his ration before we arrived. This evening we ate the last piece of bread and I realized that for the first time I was really tired. When Axel woke me for guard duty I was unable to stand up. I had to crawl around the fire for half an hour before I was able to rise.

Logjam across the Torpy River.

Day Five:

At 4:00 a.m this morning, Axel, Hilding and I went to finish the raft while Hurtig and Aage packed our equipment, so by nine o'clock we were ready to go. We were excited and wondered—could the raft carry us? It did, and we found that the big log carried more than the five other logs combined. After drifting just a short distance we found a cabin on the left bank of the river [J.B. Hooker's upriver trapping and guiding cabin] so we poled the raft to shore and entered the cabin, which was empty and devoid of food, except for a jar of fat that we took. We also took along some boards, which must have been brought upriver by motor boat. This made us realize that the river was navigable downstream.

Down we went with the raft. A couple of us poled while the others sat and watched the view. As we drifted, a calf moose came to the water's edge to drink and Axel shot it. This gave us some necessary meat along with the salt and fat to fry it. We made camp on the right side of the river and had moose liver for dinner. Had we not got the moose we would have gone to bed on empty stomachs. I guess we must be getting used to the woods because tonight we are not putting out a guard, even though we are camped right on a game trail.

Day Six:

At 5:00 a.m this morning we were up eating moose meat and then it was back on the river. We were in good spirits, so we sang songs together. Hurtig, who is in a much better mood now that we are finished with the walking, even sang some German songs he had learned during his time in Germany. We drifted for a few hours and then came upon a cabin on the left side of the river [Jim Hooker's Slide Cabin]. Nobody was there, but we found flour, baking powder, sugar and coffee. Axel bega making pancakes at once and they were the best pancakes I have ever eaten. When we left the cabin we took some baking powder, flour and coffee with us and left five dollars with my name and address.

This afternoon a cabin emerged on the right side of

Resting at Shorty Haynes' cabin.

the river; it was empty except for some traps. It probably belongs to the same trapper, as they have cabins about a day's walk apart from each other. A little later, we went through some white water and the raft ended up sitting on some rocks. Hilding and I had to jump into the river in order to break the raft free. Just a short distance downriver we went through some more white water and found a dam on the side of the river. We noticed where the beavers had cut the trees in order to float them downstream to the dam. We didn't see any beavers—maybe the trapper caught all of them.

We drifted along and came to a small rapid where the river dropped. We had to pole hard to get to shore before we went into it. This forced us to walk along the riverbank so we could assess the danger level of this rough water. Once we decided to go through, Hurtig took a picture of us, but we were on the far side of the river so we may not show up in the photo. Just below the rapids we made camp and Axel made pancakes while the rest of us made beds of spruce boughs, which are soft and warm to lie on. Dinner was moose meat, pancakes and coffee; the pancakes and coffee sure tasted the best. We were in good spirits except for the tobacco being wet; we rolled some cigarettes but they were too wet to burn. Finally we were forced to dry our tobacco by the campfire.

Day Seven:

This morning at 9:00 a.m we drifted to where the river from the north enters [Walker Creek] so we knew where we were—about fifteen miles from the Fraser River and the railway station. We hoped to reach the station by 3:00 p.m. when the train from the east arrived.

There is another cabin at the spot where the river from the north enters [Trapper Ernest Jensen's cabin]. There was no one living there, but we found some dried apples and ate a bit while we rested. A short distance downriver we came upon another cabin with smoke coming from the stovepipe. [Trapper Emmet "Shorty" Haynes' cabin, which has since been washed away by the river.] We did not bother to stop for fear of missing the train. We couldn't complain about the speed of the raft, as we were making good time, but it was hard work to keep the raft in the middle of the river.

All at once we came around a bend in the river and there was a logjam in front of us. We hit with such force that Axel flew into the river and disappeared, but he soon came up again and caught hold of the logjam. For a moment the raft began to swing around and it seemed that Axel would get crushed between it and the jam, but Hilding grabbed him and pulled him back on the raft just before it hit the jam. That was our last bit of bad fortune. A little later we came to a place where men were logging and dumping logs in the river so they would float down to a sawmill. Suddenly we were surprised when a riverboat came around a bend heading up the river. The man running it seemed just as surprised as we were. He waved and kept on going. [Probably trapper Jim Hooker.]

Soon after that, we drifted out into the Fraser River where the current was so strong we had trouble trying to get across. It had been our intention to float the Fraser River back to Sinclair Mills, but we ran out of time. Suddenly we were again surprised when a riverboat with two men came up and stopped. They had travelled upriver about a hundred kilometres from Sinclair Mills searching for us. They gave us a box of food and told us the police were involved in the search because we were four days overdue. We let the raft drift away and we walked the two kilometres to Kidd Station where we phoned the police to let them know we were safe.

Painting by Per Thomassen.

At last we were aboard the train and heading back to Sinclair Mills; a ragged-looking, unshaven bunch with torn clothes. At 5:30 that afternoon we arrived back at Sinclair Mills where the entire mill crew turned up at the station to see us. They laughed at us and we laughed back. It was good to be home after our danger-filled trip.

We didn't work the next day, because we had to rest up after our seven-day summer holiday, so we took our canoe and went fishing. We like to fish a creek near a cabin we have restored so we can live in it. The mosquitoes are so bad that we wish we were back on the Clearwater (Torpy) River where the frost seems to keep them under control.

Note: These five men had intended to raft the Fraser River back to Sinclair Mills. Unknown to them, the infamous Grand Canyon—reputed to have taken about two hundred lives—was waiting for them ninety kilometres (fifty-six miles) downriver from the point where they entered the Fraser River. Had they continued with the raft trip it is probable that they would have perished in this mighty canyon.

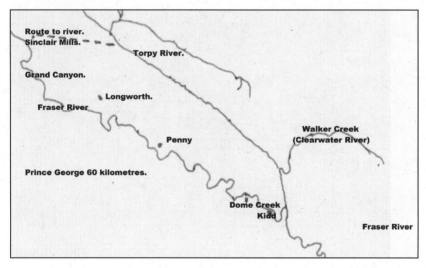

Map of Torpy River.

FREIGHTERS

Of all the people that helped develop the wilderness areas of this province, the freighters, also known as river-hogs, deserve a great deal of credit. Some of these men received little credit for the dangerous work they performed. In the years dating back to 1920, poling was the method used to move boats along the Crooked, Parsnip, Finlay and adjacent rivers. Jack Corless, who was raised in the Prince George area, recalls the history of those areas and one of the stories that survived. It seems that trapper Buck Buchanon was

An enormous amount of supplies on the bank of the Finlay River.
COURTESY ANDY MILLER

poling along the Crooked River when he noticed "Seven-fingered Gus" Dahlstrom in another boat. What was unusual was that Gus was moving along the waterway but he wasn't poling. Buck was astonished when he learned that Gus had a two and a half horse-power motor pushing his craft. He had cut the back point off and put a fir block in its place to hold the kicker, as it was called.

That was the start of what became freighting along that se-ries of waterways. From that humble beginning, well-constructed riverboats were soon plying huge loads from Summit Lake to Fort Ware.

The Hudson's Bay Company (HBC) called bids for the Fort Ware run and Lars Strom of Prince George won the contract. On one of his first trips along the Crooked River, in fact, probably at Scoville Bar

Corless boats and fifty thousand dollars in baled furs.
COURTESY JACK CORLESS

where the Pack River runs into the Parsnip River, disaster struck. Due to a lack of qualified rivermen, the boat was submerged and all the freight destroyed. HBC immediately cancelled Lars' contract.

At that point one of Lars' helpers, a huge man named Jorgy Jorgenson got the contract and hired a carpenter named Jack Duncan to build his boats. This was in the late 1920s. I have found a statement in the archives that Jack Duncan was the origi-nal designer of what came to be known as the Corless boat design. But in all fairness the honour should go to "Seven-fingered Gus." According to his namesake Jack "Duncan" Corless, others may have taken kinks out of the design, but Gus was the originator and inspiration behind it.

Many of the early-day outboard motors were unreliable be-yond belief. So when a Johnson eight-horsepower motor came along that would run most of the time, it was an instant hit. Soon a mountain of fuel and supplies was moving through the Finlay River system. By 1930, boats were taking 680 kilograms (1,500 pounds) per trip through Deserters Canyon.

I hope the reader will allow me to digress for a moment because Jack Corless has a story about Baldy Hughes that I thoroughly enjoy. Baldy drove stagecoaches with Al Young along the Blackwater Road for many years. Hence what was originally known as Moose Springs was changed to Baldy Hughes when he purchased that piece of land. In due course he left the area and moved into Prince George, letting his land go for back taxes. In turn, the land was picked up by Jack Corless' namesake, Jack Duncan. As fate played out the cards, Jack Corless inherited it after Duncan's death. Then a strange thing happened. Jack was delivering fuel down in the Interior when he met a man named Glenn Hall who told him that he had a contract to build a radar base on the Blackwater Road. When told where, Jack realized it was on the property he was inheriting from Duncan. He kept his peace and in due course went to the site to find buildings under construction and the Dome going up. To really cap things, they had put in concrete foundations, which meant Jack now owned the buildings as well. After seeing this Jack gave Glenn the good news, that he owned the property. Then he rushed to town to push for the will to be probated so it would be in his name. Just in time it went through.

Fleet of Corless boats on the Pack River.
COURTESY CHERRY CORLESS

What a mess for the big boy from Ottawa who claimed it was government land. He came to Jack's office with five accomplices and tried to bully him into submission. The end result— the land that had been bought at a tax sale for $425 changed hands for $4,500.

Getting back to the rivers, one of the first employees taken on by Jorgenson with his new HBC contract was Dick Corless. His father, R.F. Corless Sr. came to Canada from Lancashire in 1911. His wife was to follow on the ill-fated *Titanic*, but fate stepped in with some good luck/bad luck when baby Edwin caught pneumonia and the trip was delayed. They came to Canada on the next voyage a few months later where they met Dick in Saskatchewan. In 1913 Dick and his dear friend Jack Duncan travelled by train to Ashcroft and then by stage to Fort George. Their stage driver was the famous Al Young who, along with alternate driver Baldy Hughes, manned the stages for many years.

As stated, Dick Corless Jr. began his stint as a riverman working with Jorgy Jorgenson, who had the contract hauling freight for the Hudson's Bay Company from Summit Lake to Fort Ware. Art van Somer and Del Miller often assisted in these ventures as we shall see later on.

In 1936 Jorgy and Dick were in the process of unloading their riverboats at Fort Ware when tragedy struck; Jorgy was packing a forty-five-kilogram (one-hundred-pound) bag of flour from the boat when he suffered a heart attack and died. Dick brought his body back to Prince George and in due course applied for this same contract. His application was accepted and thus began his twenty-year span of river adventures.

Fort McLeod.
COURTESY THE EXPLORATION PLACE P977.4.3

Freight boats in the shallow Crooked River.
COURTESY CHERRY CORLESS

During the early years of freighting, and prior to the construction of the highway to the Parsnip River Bridge in 1952, Dick had to haul freight right from Summit Lake through the shallow Crooked River. Since the rivers were always free of ice well before the lakes, Dick came up with a great equalizing idea. He used to scrounge all the wood ashes he could find and spread them across the lake from his freight pick-up point to where the river exited the lake. The black ashes drew the sun's heat and opened a channel across the lake well ahead of the normal opening time.

At one point along the Crooked River a bunch of rocks protruded up out of the water. As they reminded the river rats of a bunch of bums pointing up in the air, the place won the title of Scatter-ass Riffle. Every little bit of humour was used wherever and whenever possible as it added so much to the colour and interest of the trips; after a week constantly on the river anything of human interest helped enormously. One thing all these men agreed on was that there is no colder place on earth than an open riverboat in late fall. One can dress for minus forty degrees Celsius and still be tormented by hypothermia.

Through trial and error, the men turned what originally had been tubs that tipped over at the slightest movement into stable boats capable of carrying huge loads through wild water, while drawing only inches of water. Many minor changes of design took place, such as making the stern of the boat quite narrow, which allowed it to turn sharply in narrow, wild streams. Through the many years that Corless and the van Somers used these riverboats, not one drowning took place. Although much of the credit goes to the experience and water sense of these men, I believe the safety record was for the most part due to the brilliant design of these boats.

Dick used two riverboats with inboard engines and the rest were all outboard engines. The two inboard motors proved more than competitive with the outboard motors. For instance, while the outboards used about four barrels or 180 gallons of gas for a round trip, the inboards made it on about two and a half drums. The trip to Fort Ware, later renamed Ware, usually took five days, while the return trip took two days.

Dick was a jack-of-all-trades and one does not have to peruse many old newspapers to find where he was involved in one deal

Dick Corless and four wolves.
COURTESY CHERRY CORLESS

or another. A memorable story of one venture he missed out on is worth recalling. Apparently he got an invitation from a friend to join him in buying a parcel of land near Prince George. His half of the asking price was $12,000. No small amount of money at that time, but according to his friend, it was a steal at that. Perhaps Dick relied on the old saying "if it looks too good to be true, it probably is" because he turned down the offer. Apparently Dick was astounded a few years later to learn that his friend had sold $450,000 worth of gravel and still owned the property. This spot later became the PGE Industrial site. It appears that Lady Luck knocked on Dick's door that day and he wasn't home to answer.

Al Thorpe of Prince George was a close friend to Dick and to-gether they constructed and sold several different sizes and versions of the Corless boat to companies in the Interior. This was during 1957–58. Their price was $10 per running foot or $360 for a 36-foot boat. It strikes me that the price has gone up a bit since then. Old-timers may recall that Al was also a member of the Hub City 4, a band that played on CKPG Radio for several years.

After twenty years on the rivers, Dick sold out the freighting

Riverman Harvey Simms rides in the bow, while Art van Somers and Louie Toma sit at the stern.   Deserters Peak in background.
COURTESY AL THORPE

business to Art van Somers and went to work for Frank McMann, the man who ran Westcoast Transmission. Dick's main function was to guide bankers, governors or other elite along the river on fishing or hunting trips. Acting as a promoter, Dick was designated a foreman-at-large, which meant that he just roamed around and did whatever he wanted as long as he made these people happy.

The mission was to loosen their purse strings and help finance the oil pipeline. With this objective in mind, Dick built a houseboat which was launched at the Parsnip Bridge and then towed to Cut Thumb Creek one hundred kilometres (sixty-two miles) down-river. Capable of sleeping six people, it had all the amenities of home. With two riverboats stationed at Summit Lake, Dick would ferry people back and forth to the houseboat.

Jack Corless and Bill van Somer, 1937. COURTESY JACK CORLESS

Al Thorpe had a few other special memories of Dick that he was willing to share. Such as the time one of Dick's guests caught a large bull trout right beside the houseboat. After a hearty meal of said fish, Dick informed the participants that the big fish they had just consumed had spent the entire summer parked beside the houseboat, eating all the goodies that came out of the septic system. It's hard to believe that in spite of such treatment, Dick managed to raise all the money needed for the pipeline.

In the fall of 1957 when Dick and Al went to tow the houseboat back to Summit Lake for the winter they found it high and dry. The river had dropped considerably and this left the men with a lot of shovelling before it reached deep water again.

Dick's boundless sense of humour came to the fore at Ken and Kathy Melville's lodge on Tudyah Lake. It seems that Kathy was in the process of preparing breakfast for a group when she stated, "It must be at least thirty-five below zero today!"

Instantly Dick came back with, "I know and it makes me wonder how cold it is outside."

Dick's houseboat high and dry at Cut Thumb Creek.
COURTESY AL THORPE

I got a kick out of some of their sayings, such as, "Never eat yellow snow." Or, "There is nothing in the world as sexy as a woman chewing and spitting snuff."

It seems that the head honcho on the pipeline, Frank McMann, was a character in his own right. On one of their fundraising trips to London, England, his party set up shop in a display room. They didn't have a suit among the bunch so in order to put up a good front, they rented some suits. After the presentation was over, all the party had to sleep on the floor of that room because they didn't have enough money for a hotel room.

Dick's sense of humour displayed itself quite well the time they were in the midst of a party when he brought an elderly prospector home, and with a great deal of effort, sat him in a chair. With even more difficulty, they managed to stuff a drink into his hand. The crazy part of this deal was that the prospector had frozen to death a few days earlier.

Dick's sense of humour was evident many times through the years, such as the time he went along the river putting up arrows pointing in all directions. Followers and first-time travellers were found heading in all directions, until they realized what was going on and ignored the arrows.

Another name that often echoed along the northern waterways was Del Miller, a man who did a great deal of trapping and freighting along the Finlay River.

Del was born near Windsor, Ontario, and a short time later his parents moved to the US. By the time 1910 rolled around young Del got restless and headed north in search of adventure. Arriving in Prince George, he made his way through Giscome Portage and on to Hudson's Hope. For several years he hauled mail from Fort St. John to Hudson's Hope, by dogsled in winter and then by canoe in summer.

During 1934 he and adventurer, trapper and prospector Carl Davidson of Prince George were hired to help Art and Don van Somer move fuel and freight from Summit Lake to Fort Ware. This involved a river trip of 418 kilometres (260 miles) one way.

During that same summer two young lads fresh from the University of Alberta travelled the waterways north from Prince George by canoe. Their names were Len Wilson and Joe Prest. Their mission was adventure and the hope of finding gold along the Finlay River. As with so many who went before them, their trip was long on adventure, but short on gold.

Although they worked many sandbars, they had little luck as far as getting any amount of gold. They did, however, certainly have their share of exciting adventure. During the summer of 1934 they spent a lot of time riding with Del and Don Miller

Picture of Del Miller, c 1940.
COURTESY ANDY MILLER

in their forty-four-foot riverboat. As well, Len kept a journal of their travels. In preparation for one of their trips through Deserters Canyon in high water the journal noted:

I studied the river carefully today and I'm sure we couldn't have gotten up it even with an empty canoe. Don shot a moose tonight so we are going to be well fed. We had to get up before daylight to pack the meat in before it got warm. It was near three miles away so we certainly were ready for breakfast on our return at 6:00 a.m.

When Del moved the boat up to the canyon, the first thing we did was pack the canoe and our stuff over the portage and make camp upstream. Del and his family were guests of Gus Trapp and his wife. [Gus had a cabin near the canyon.] Joe, by means of an ingenious twisted string, roasted a nice piece of moose meat. It sure was good. Summer moose meat is a lot like beef. We walked through part of the canyon. It is a wild and lovely place with exciting stretches of water.

Next day we began packing Del's supplies over. He had several Trapper Nelson pack boards; I have never seen any better. The first trips we packed one hundred pounds and then added a twenty-five-pound box, usually dried fruit or prunes, for a top load. We found this to be okay.

It was great to be young and strong. We were in no great hurry as the water was still too high for Del to tackle the canyon, even with an empty boat. Each trip took near forty minutes, and after each three trips Del had a good pot of bush tea ready. I don't know how many tons of stuff Del had but we got it all over and had a day or two to loaf and fish. Joe made a nice baking of bread in the oven at Gus Trapps'. We had more rain and a rummy day. [The men often played rummy or bridge while waiting for the river to co-operate.]

Next day Del sized up the river and said, 'We'll try it.' He had it well figured out from past experience. We had loaded three good poles and a big coil of rope. Del had tied a barrel of gas in the bow and we started off with Del at the motor, while Don, Joe and I could do little but cheer through the first part. Del got out in the big eddy and picked up speed as he swung around. We hit the bottom of the canyon at full speed but the fast water soon slowed us down. For the first one hundred yards it was nip and tuck, but we ground along just barely making headway. Del kept moving the bow to probe for any weakness in the current, but there wasn't any.

We reached the first drop and Del inched the boat into shore and the three of us (super cargo) jumped out with the coil of rope, which was tied to the bow. We moved up to a big rock about one hundred yards ahead and got set. Then Del eased into the current with us straining on the rope, the motor roaring and Del cheering, we edged the boat up on the first step. He got into a favourable eddy, moved up and we boarded again.

This time we stood poised with our poles. When we hit the second chute, the boat stood still for a moment, and then we were able to push and very gradually got up the incline where we were able to move upstream. The water was rougher and really kicked the boat around, but it wasn't as hard-going as in the fast hard water we had come through. We were soon up to the big hay stacks [rollers] at the head of the canyon. The current here was very fast and Del had to take advantage of an eddy below the rollers and cut across the bottom of them. The bow hit the lower roller and even with the forty-five gallons of gas in the bow, the boat was thrown ten or twelve feet in the air. It was sure lucky the barrel was tied in. Then we were through and it was the most exciting boat ride I've ever had.

I disagree with the writer that it was luck that made Del tie the barrel in the front of the boat; I think it was deliberate and the result of lessons learned the hard way. Otherwise, I sure like his description of Del tackling Deserters Canyon!

Another interesting entry in Len's journal describes freighting along the Finlay River with an eight-horse Johnson motor:

> Freighters like Del can push a four-ton load from Finlay Forks to Fort Graham, but only two and one half tons from Fort Graham to Fort Ware. If Deserters Canyon is in high water, then the load has to be portaged over a one half-mile ridge. Medium-high water allows about a half-ton load through the canyon, providing you have men and lines to line up about one hundred yards of fast water in two places.

It appears that time was almost meaningless on these trips. The old saying "Hurry up and wait" was certainly in use when dealing with rivers and floodwaters. What was doubly important was that Len took a great number of pictures which were given to Del's son, Andy, just a few years ago. Sometimes Len climbed the cliffs at Deserters Canyon to get better shots of the freighters moving their boats through the rough water. Many years later, the pictures and journal Len Wilson wrote during his trip in the early 1930s were sent to Del's son Andy. With deep gratitude, I have been given the honour to use the journal and pictures as I see fit.

The need for lining through the fast water is better understood when we realize that Del's engine only delivered eight horsepower. This meant that small loads were relayed through the rapids and then the full load taken aboard to continue along the river.

Del spent several years trapping about 125 kilometres (78 miles) upriver of Fort Graham. Later, he settled with his family along the Finlay River 40 kilometres (25 miles) south of Fort Ware. The Del Creek watershed bears testimony to the huge size of his trapline. Throughout the following years he spent a great deal of time travelling the Finlay River.

When hauling freight along the river at Deserters Canyon, some freighters portaged the supplies over a half-mile trail rather than fight the high water. Just below Deserters Rock, a whirlpool formed. Known as "Hole in the Water" to the early-day Natives, it had surprises in store for careless river travellers.

During the summer of 1934 several huge forest fires raged through the Finlay country.

Upon their return to Millerville, as Del's main cabin became known, they learned that several of their line cabins had been destroyed by fire. This meant a great deal of hard work to rebuild and stock the cabins with stoves and supplies. As well, they had to cut an enormous supply of firewood to last any long cold spell, injury or sickness. Len pointed out that the Kwadacha River was formerly known as the Whitewater River. He also claimed that the eighty-two-year-old chief at Fort Ware was named Darcy Mackenzie who claimed he was a descendant of Alexander Mackenzie.

The back of the picture shown below reads:

13/8/34. A little further upstream the boat is swinging into the 'high-water channel' and encountering the second bit of fast water in the canyon. Don is running forward to poke the bow away from the rock while Art crouches down in front of the load out of Del's line of sight, with his weight thrust back helping to keep the propeller under water.

COURTESY ANDY MILLER

Another tidbit of information concerned the Ne-parle-pas Rapids. According to Len it was originally called the "La rapide qui ve parle pas" (they do not speak), because the rapids did not have the usual roar associated with rapids.

I found it interesting that Del and many of the other trappers would trap one side of their main watershed one winter and then the other side the following winter. This was their method of preventing over-trapping. Some of these lines were so long that the trappers never got to visit the far end of them which often ended in rock mountains that supported little in the way of furs.

The back of the picture shown below reads:

13/8/34. 1:45 p.m.. Here you can see Del (at the engine) and Carl running up the second stretch of lining in Deserters Canyon. Carl has just given a thrust with his pole. Jor [Jorgy Jorgensen] is onshore, hauling on the rope. We jokingly remark that the engineers try to pull these kickers [outboard engines] up these extra fast places by the tail. We are now working with two boats, Art and Don [van Somer] being in the other. Joe, Linquist and myself, each man a lining rope.

COURTESY ANDY MILLER

Len spent two years with Del and it was during their second winter together that they made a surprising discovery—Del's father and Len's maternal grandmother were brother and sister. Imagine meeting only a few people and finding a relative out in the middle of nowhere. Sometimes it truly is a small world. Finally, after two years of adventure, when the summer turned to fall, Len paddled his canoe out to Peace River and went home to Edmonton. His good friend Joe stayed to spend the winter trapping with Del Miller.

That same October, the Bedaux expedition that had been trav-

The back of the picture shown below reads:

13/8/34. Now they are heading up the "high-water channel." Just ahead of the boat is a pitch so steep that it is necessary to help the engine with a rope to shore from the bow. In the smooth water between the rocks at the left you can see the splash of the rope. Carl stands braced taking it in as fast as he can. When the boat is well away again, the bowman will quickly break the knot by jerking on a false end, then a second stop is not required. There are six bits of fast water, three of which require this lining operation.

COURTESY ANDY MILLER

elling through Northern BC aborted their challenging trip when they encountered half a metre (two feet) of snow in Sifton Pass. Del and Carl Davidson were among several boats hired to bring all the members back to Hudson's Hope. In among the archives is Bedaux's payment of $180 to Del for twenty days work. For himself and his boat and motor, Del got the exciting amount of $9 a day. This was a great sum of money at a time when wages were $2 a day.

Prince George resident Vern Gogolin has a rather cute story involving Del Miller. During early summer 1955, Del used his riverboat to haul their crew of surveyors from the Parsnip River Bridge north along the river to different location spots. After that work was finished, Del was hired on as an axe-man to cut survey lines in the Pine Pass for the PGE Railway. One day they were coming back to the lodge a bit early so they decided to climb up a mountain to Hart Lake, which at that time had no road access. Before they reached the lake, Vern was lagging behind so the party-chief, Keith Crow, chided him by referring to Del, "You're being out-walked by a seventy-year-old man."

Johnson OK 15. A reliable outboard motor.
COURTESY VERN GOGOLIN

Vern didn't let on until they reached the lodge that he had turned an ankle that same morning, but when he had trouble getting his boot off the party-chief sort of apologized for kidding him about Del. As it turned out he didn't have to because Vern knew that Del was sure in good shape for his age. It was all steep side-hill walking in that area and consequently very easy to turn an ankle.

Some may wonder why there were so many elderly people working in the woods in those days. The answer, aside from them wanting to be there, is that there was no pension available until one reached the age of seventy. Without a nest egg, people were often forced to continue working even though their health may have dictated otherwise.

Vern added another tidbit about this man: one spring Del took his riverboat and hauled freight up Tacheeda Creek to Tacheeda Lake, a trip that involved jumping beaver dams. Those who have seen this stream will wonder how that was possible, but he certainly did it. One way or another they always managed to get the freight through.

As mentioned, another river-hog who worked that run was Art van Somer, who became an expert in river travel at a young age. Already back in the early 1930s he was so acknowledged as a riverboat operator that he was hired on with the Bedaux expedition in its failed attempt to cross the Northern Rockies from Edmonton

Ludwig Smasslet with Del Miller's children, c 1940. He once walked 130 kilometres (81 miles) in two days to get a supply of tobacco.
COURTESY ANDY MILLER

A good load—twenty drums of fuel.
COURTESY JACK CORELESS

to the west coast of BC. In due course, Art and his son Bob took over from Dick Corless, hauling food, fuel and supplies from Prince George to Fort Ware. The portion they ran by boat was from the Parsnip River Bridge north of Prince George to Fort Ware, a distance of 418 kilometres (260 miles). Bob worked that run from 1954 until 1968 when Williston Lake flooded the area.

I questioned Bob as to the size of loads they took in these boats and he recalled taking twenty-four drums of fuel in one load.

Ed Strandburg on the Finlay River.
COURTESY STEVE MARYNOVICH

Many loads grossed out at over five tons.

Art had a year to remember when the river had such extreme high water that he had to unload all his freight and hop it up through the wild water one ton at a time. I think it is safe to say that he earned his salt by the time he moved five tons per boat through the rapids in that fashion.

When I asked Bob what his favourite memory was of that area, he recalled the meetings he used to have with the elderly trappers at the Parsnip Bridge Camp. Several memorable people used to frequent the camp, such as Hamburger Joe, Bob Isadore, Charlie Cunningham, Ed Strandburg, George McGuire and others. The stories that were handed down from early-day river travellers held

Joe Berghammer, alias Hamburger Joe, an all-round woodsman, trapper and riverman who left a legacy well-worth remembering.
THE MACKENZIE AND DISTRICT MUSEUM 2003.15.148

The van Somer houseboat on Summit Lake, 1941.
COURTESY BOB VAN SOMER

his attention for hours on end. One story that has survived the ages was when wilderness wanderer Hamburger Joe walked over 100 kilometres (62 miles) to get tobacco. In a similar vein, Ludwig Smasslet also walked 130 kilometres (81 miles) for the same purpose. These men often paid a high price for their daring. As an example, Ludwig's brother Ivor was killed in a snowslide in 1939 at the tender age of eighteen.

Hamburger Joe became a legend along the chain of rivers for his courage in amputating his own frozen toes. Many different stories have evolved as to how it happened, but a man who shared his room in a logging camp told me that he was caught out on his trapline when the weather turned extremely cold and his feet were frozen before he reached his cabin. Joe added that during the surgery he passed in and out of consciousness several times.

For many years a man named Ben Corke ran the trading post at Ingenika. As was often the case, Natives used to camp at his place and stay with him. Apparently Ben decided it was time to get them to move on. Unknown to the Natives, Ben had a peg leg, and one evening he put it to good use. Just as they were going to bed he took off his leg and threw it into the corner of the cabin. Then he started twisting on his head as if he were unscrewing it. At the same instant he blew out the light and left the rest to their imaginations. It worked. The Natives stayed clear of this strange individual who could dismantle his body at will.

Fort Graham closed down in 1948 and Fort Ware stayed open until 1952. Throughout those years an enormous amount of supplies were transported along the rivers. When Ben Corke left Ingenika, Art van Somers ran it until it closed.

Bob states that his worst memories were the attempts made by government officials to hoodwink the trappers in the Finlay area. He personally drove a BC Hydro representative named Charlie Cunningham around in his riverboat to meet with the trappers and recalls the fairy tales that he heard Cunningham deliver to a trusting, hard-working group of people who had their entire livelihoods destroyed by the creation of Williston Lake. The promises were astounding: there would be resorts galore all around the lake area; commercial fishing would bring employment and money to the area. Some of the people such as the McDougals and Strandburgs did not want to sell. Pressure was continuous and successful; Bob claims these two families told him that their payoff was less than the value of their buildings, let alone their livelihoods.

When Bob's brother, Jim, sold his trapline to BC Hydro he picked up the cheque in Vancouver, immediately went to a bank and cashed it, bought a briefcase and put the money in it, and then caught the first Greyhound bus back to Prince George as he didn't have full faith in the people he was dealing with. Apparently the cash felt good in his pocket.

I hope I don't give the impression that I was against the Peace River dams, it is just that I wish it could have been done in a better manner so it didn't leave thousands of moose to drown in the tree-strewn lake. One witness I talked with said he watched a moose as it jumped out over several trees that were jammed against the lakeshore. As with other moose, it made it out into the open lake, but then it could not find a place to get back out again. It swam around until it went down.

Getting back to my interview with Bob van Somer, I asked about the amount of game they spotted along the rivers and he pointed out that he used to see between 200 and 250 moose a day on his trips along the river, especially in the fall during the rut. As well, though they seldom ever spotted grizzlies, there was always an abundance of black bears.

This fit in so well with my own experiences—in all the years I travelled the Fraser River through good grizzly territory I saw the grand total of one grizzly from my boat. I know they followed the rivers a lot in spring, often searching for moose calves, but obviously they managed to just keep back out of sight. I have spotted hundreds of black bears from my boat. Of course the fact that grizzlies blend into the foliage much easier than blacks had a bearing on it.

Bob recalls the huge grizzly tracks he ran into in fresh snow while working with some surveyors near the Nation River. He stood with both of his boots inside of one hind foot track left by the bear. It just took one glance for the entire crew to agree to de-part the area; but that was not the end of the story. A short time later Bob ran into the same huge tracks walking in the snow along the edge of a road almost one hundred kilometres (sixty-two miles) from where they first came upon its tracks. Two of the group of surveyors then stumbled upon its carcass. There was nothing left but the frame of what had once been a huge grizzly. It had starved to death, its teeth rotted away, which explains why it had stayed out in the winter rather than go to its den.

At this point I must bring Jerry Witter into the picture. A cousin of Bob van Somer, he enjoyed riding along on the trips to Fort Ware. Jerry came from pioneer stock, and has some memo-ries from his father that deserve to be kept for posterity. In the fall of 1923 his father and mother, Hank and Marg, were headed for the Parsnip River to spend the winter trapping. Upon arriving at McLeod Lake they were informed that trappers were already in that area. This forced them to change plans and head for the Phillips Creek country where they spent the years until 1948 trap-ping in the winters and prospecting during the summers. On the long trek into that area, Marg refused to ride on the horses and so walked the entire distance. That hang-up came to an end when she learned just how much work was involved in walking. Within a short period of time she adapted and then it was difficult to keep her off the horses.

Gold had shown up in bars along the river and this led Hank

and his brother to find a novel way to get it. With only a homemade wheelbarrow, and blasting powder, along with picks and shovels, they exerted an enormous amount of energy digging a trench over two metres deep and 150 metres long. Their objective was to by-pass a portion of the creek and get at the bars without having to contend with the water. Weirs were built to force the water off into the ditch, but when extreme high water came it took the weirs and all, down the creek and that was the end of that idea. Years of back-breaking work had gone for nothing, which was often the case with prospectors. When gold was discovered in that area many years later Jerry told his dad that he had been on the right track but didn't go deep enough. He then added that the mine had hit pay dirt at a depth of 90 metres (295 feet). This led his father to reply, "If we'd have known it was down there we would have dug for it."

One day when they were nearing completion of the trench a man came along on a horse and joined them in having coffee.

He stared at the trench for the longest time and finally asked, "Did you fellows dig that trench."

"Yes," Hank replied.

"Where's your machinery?"

"Don't have any; just the tools and wheelbarrow."

"Are you fellows telling me that you dug that trench by hand?"

"Yes, that's right!"

Whereupon the man threw the cup of coffee into the creek, got on his horse and left without another word.

Jerry added a touch to the story by saying that he went to that spot many years later and the trench was still evident.

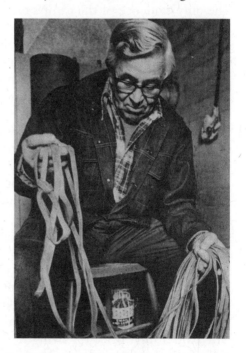

Hank Witter with babiche for making snowshoes.
COURTESY JERRY WITTER

In response I told Jerry that his dad was but one of many that left signs all over the wilderness of aborted mining ventures. Such as the large cave along Williams Creek near Barkerville that goes about twenty metres (sixty-six feet) into the solid rock and almost high enough to stand up in. One can but wonder how many months or years were put into the hope of finding gold in that solid rock. At least Hank Witter got some gold from his venture. Sometimes the two men panned out an ounce a day.

Jerry added another piece of history possibly lost long ago. He described how a split-off group of Natives left Ingenika and headed northwest where they set up a camp near what is now Blackpine Lake. For a short period of time they even had a school there. During January 1997 Jerry helped set up a camp for Finlay Forest Industries on the same spot and they even used the septic system from the school, which was still in working order. Since then the settlement of Blackpine has dissolved into the dustbin of history. The only evidence of the camp's existence is a clearing that is rapidly going back to nature.

Jerry's brother, Bill Witter, left his own story to be told and retold along the chain of rivers. His alarm clock had given up the ghost so while in Prince George he had purchased a new one. They were camped along the river the next evening when Bill wound his new clock, set the alarm for 4:30 a.m. and then retired for the night. When the hour arrived, the most ear-splitting racket echoed through the northern woods. Unable to bear the racket, Bill leapt out of his sleeping bag and fumbled again and again in a futile attempt to find the alarm shut-off. Then, amid a lot of cussing, there was splash and then "glub, glub, glub," the sound of a new alarm clock going underwater.

~

Harry Chingee of McLeod Lake spent many years travelling the Finlay and Parsnip Rivers. He worked at many different projects including guiding, which he certainly learned to love. He and his wife paid a high price for living in remote areas, in that they lost two of their children, but with their stoic outlook on life, took it all in stride. Harry acquired a vast amount of experience including a ten-year stint as chief of the McLeod Lake First Nation Band.

When asked to relate some of his experiences he didn't seem to know where to begin. But he got going when I asked if he ever had any problems with grizzlies during his many years in the woods. It turned out that he had to shoot two grizzlies when they attacked him. In one case his hunter had wounded a moose and they spent hours trailing it. Suddenly a grizzly jumped out of the bushes right at them. Harry shot it and then wasn't sure whether the bear was after them or the moose. The bear may have picked up the blood trail and perhaps they were all trailing the moose. It is easier to understand that they were in bear territory when we learn that his guiding area includes the Misinchinka River, Colboure Creek and Renolds Creek, all good grizzly country.

Harry Chingee and picture of himself with a boom of logs on the Finlay River.

Harry has mixed feelings about the Williston Reservoir. He feels that it should have been done with less damage to the environment. He spent several years laying out cut blocks for Cattermole Construction and so developed strong feelings for that area. He also gained a wealth of knowledge about logging, having spent two years falling trees, and four years studying forestry in school. It was all put to good use throughout the years he worked in the forest industry.

Many of Harry's pictures were taken around campfires and I think that speaks for itself and makes it more understandable when he says, "I liked logging and the other jobs I had, but I loved guiding best of all because there is such excitement and beauty out in the mountains."

Harry Chingee's brothers, Sam and Alec, at one of their guiding camps.

One of his more memorable hunts was the time he set an American hunter up on two grizzlies in three days. Both times the hunter got away close shots at the bears and both times he missed clean. He didn't have to tell Harry why he missed; the answer was obvious when he couldn't stop his rifle from shaking violently. There was another exciting moment when he and a friend were walking through the woods and they saw something white coming toward them. It turned out to be a sow grizzly with three yearlings. They stopped just a few feet away, where the sow looked them over, gave a couple coughs and led her yearlings away at a gallop. Although the charge had only taken a few seconds, Harry was astounded to find that his partner was about nine metres (thirty feet) up in a tree.

Harry seems unable to accept the death of one of his friends after he was attacked by a grizzly bear. Harry cannot accept the fact that Harvey Cardinal tracked a grizzly bear in the snow and the bear got him from behind. He states that he has thought it over a great deal and believes that Harvey was too good a hunter to be taken that way. As it was about minus forty degrees, Harry thinks there was a good chance that Harvey's rifle froze up. There is also the probability that because of the extreme cold, that he had his ears covered which restricted his hearing for the few seconds it took for the attack to be successful. Once again, the bear was sick or it wouldn't have been out in such severe weather. Its agony and hunger must have made it all the more mean and prone to attack.

Several times I asked these rivermen, including Harry, how they managed to keep warm travelling the rivers in their open boats during late autumn. Their answers were always the same— they didn't. Truly, I doubt that there is a colder place on earth than running the rivers on a cold, damp morning. The cold seems to settle in our bones.

Looking back at the creation of Williston Lake, it wasn't just the moose that had trouble in the new-forming lake.

On June 13, 1969 the Prince George *Citizen* ran a big headline:

FOUR LOGGERS RESCUED
FROM WILLISTON LAKE

Four men were rescued from Williston Lake this morning after spending forty hours in the water hanging on to a tree, their overturned boat and a log. No one knew they were missing until their 7:00 a.m. rescue today. For John Beaudet, twenty-four; Dennis Spoklie, twenty-five; his brother Ralph, twenty-three and Wayne McVeigh, all of Sinclair Mills, Friday June 13 started out as an ominous day. At dawn today, they had been in the water since 3:00 p.m. Wednesday...

"Friday the 13th is supposed to be an unlucky day but it sure turned out lucky for us," said Dennis.

The four men had been contract-falling timber for a private contractor. They had a good supply of food and were not expected out for some time, consequently they were completely on their own and no one would have missed them for weeks. Anyway, they were making their way along the lake when they ran into rough water about sixteen kilometres (ten miles) north of Finlay Forks. As the storm went from bad to worse, Dennis felt compelled to get out of the open lake where his boat was taking a terrible beating. At one point he hit a piece of driftwood so hard that it cracked the transom. Possibly this had a bearing on the boat rolling over, as water may have leaked in under the false floor. Finally Dennis decided to get out of the tree-strewn lake and into the surrounding flooded area.

Dennis Spoklie—a hero by any standard of measurement.

The idea worked, because once they got into the trees, the huge waves subsided, although the swells were still rising and falling. The men are not certain as to exactly what happened, but it appears that the back of the boat caught on the limb of a tree, not allowing the boat to rise with a swell. Instantly the boat filled with water and overturned, dumping all their supplies into the lake. Only a sleeping bag was retained and it proved to be Wayne's salvation, warmth-wise. Three of the men got into the trees, while Wayne stayed on the nose of the boat which was still above water.

What to do? The men did not see any options available to them. The water was icy cold so swimming was out of the question. Staying in the trees was their only hope, but how long could they hang there without tiring and falling into the water? Besides, there would be no search because no one knew their whereabouts. Through the first long night the men constantly talked to each other in order to keep their spirits up. A strong wind was dissipating their body heat at an alarming rate, until they came up with a brilliant idea—they stuffed their shirts full of green leaves off the surrounding trees and that acted as insulation, protecting them from the cold.

After daylight arrived the men took stock and realized that they were certain to die if they stayed where they were. Someone had to try to reach help. Waiting was out of the question; their only hope of survival depended on what course of action they took.

Ralph slipped into one of the floatation devices and lowered himself into the water, determined to try to reach the open lake where boats could be heard going by occasionally. No sooner did he enter the water, when he found his breath taken away. Back up the tree he went, stating that he would rather die than endure that icy water. At that time we have to realize that Ralph and the other men had accepted the fact that they were doomed.

Finally Dennis made the most important decision of his entire life. He slipped into the flotation device and forced himself to swim out through the debris toward the open lake. In due course he found a floating tree and climbed up on top of it. From that spot he commanded a view of the channel where the boats travelled. Several times through that long day Dennis watched boats go by and each time he stood up on the tree and waved. The men on the boats didn't notice because their full attention was drawn to watching the channel so they wouldn't hit a floating tree or other pieces of driftwood. For Dennis, this left no hope as no one even looked in his direction.

Back in the trees, John, who was known locally as Jack, had tied himself to a tree with his belt to ensure he would not fall. After

Ralph Spoklie: "There's no doubt about it, Dennis saved our lives."

hours in that position, his legs went numb. Ralph, for his part, had a little kitten they had taken along as a mascot, and it came to good use. Although it clawed his tummy up a bit, it gave off a surprising amount of heat and helped keep him warm. Wayne, on the nose of the boat, had the sleeping bag, so he had no trouble keeping warm.

Many times throughout the second night the men called out to Dennis, who was so exhausted that he repeatedly fell off the tree into the water. Several times they assumed him dead when he did not answer their calls. In fact, he only responded a few times throughout the night.

Ralph and Jack, who had spent their second night in the trees, were having some weird experiences: airplanes circled their location; boats and cars came by but none would offer a ride; and a train came right up to the trees they were in. They were obviously hallucinating, which may have been a good thing, as Ralph

Rescue boat approaching the spot where the boat capsized.
COURTESY ALLEN SPOKLIE

states that he had accepted he was going to die and somehow it didn't seem so bad after all.

At about 7:00 a.m. the next morning a tugboat made its way along the lake. By then Dennis was so weak and filled with despair that he simply waved his hand. Lady Luck smiled down on Dennis that morning because someone on the tug just happened to glance in his direction and spotted

The overturned boat when it was recovered, July 1969.
COURTESY ALLEN SPOKLIE

him. The tugboat operator, Dan Murphy, was shocked to find a man sitting on a tree in the middle of a huge lake a hundred kilometres from nowhere. As for Dennis, we can scarcely imagine the feelings that swept over him as he saw the boat turn in his direction. When the boys back in the trees fully accepted that a boat was approaching the tears fell openly and freely. The impossible rescue had taken place.

An ambulance was summoned and rushed Dennis and Jack to Prince George Hospital where Jack's feet needed urgent attention. They had turned black and the tops of both feet had broken open and were exuding liquid at a rapid rate. Surprisingly, after a few days he was released and both feet were saved. Dennis, considering what he had been through, made a rapid recovery after his session with hypothermia.

Material rescued from the lake.
COURTESY ALLEN SPOKLIE

A few days later a diver went to the scene and recovered almost everything from the four and a half metres (fifteen feet) of water beneath the boat. In retrospect, Dennis suggests that his sixteen-foot deep hull boat with its seventy-five horsepower motor was probably overloaded. Especially when we consider the rough water that can be encountered in Williston Lake.

In a follow-up article on June 17, 1969 the *Citizen* noted:

LAKE JUST LIKE A JUNGLE

"It is unbelievable how they lived through it. It's just like a jungle in there."

The comment by Prince George scuba diver Russ Logan, describes Williston Lake where four men were rescued last Friday after their boat overturned during a squall on the man-made lake behind the WAC Bennett Dam.

Logan and a companion, Ralph McLean, spent the whole day last Saturday salvaging both the boat and the equipment lost by the survivors of the mishap. "It's beyond me how they survived." Repeated Logan. He said the point where the 1,500-lb. boat went down was like an underwater forest—a jungle of living trees, mostly poplar, that were left to drown in the waters of the huge Peace power reservoir.

Logan and McLean were commissioned to salvage what they could of the equipment lost.

Logan said the situation was aggravated by masses of floating logs and debris. Despite the perilous conditions underwater, the scuba divers recovered in eleven dives, the following equipment: one motorcycle, three rifles, five power saws, one tent, a variety of canned foods, clothing, a number of pack boards and miscellaneous equipment. The partly-submerged boat was also recovered.

Dennis recalls that he was pleasantly surprised that everything he had on the boat was recovered, except for one item, which must not have been important because he cannot remember it now.

When I interviewed Ralph, he summed up his version of the entire nightmare by saying, "There's no question about it, if Dennis had not swum out into the open lake we would have died. Dennis saved our lives."

So what was the total price that was paid for the flooded land? It may be hard to understand, but these freighters knew a freedom that cannot be explained by words. When we follow their trails after the flooding we find a trail of sorrow. Dick Corless for instance, appeared to have not been able to find anything worth living for after all those years of travelling those hundreds of miles of wilderness waterways. He moved to Vancouver Island where his health deserted him. He learned from his doctor that his back was pretty well shot and that surgery might well end in a wheelchair. His wife came home one day to find that Dick had taken his own life.

Dick was by no means alone in his failure to find meaning after the flooding took place. It had a profound effect on many people that were dependent on the industry that had built up along the waterways. Art van Somer, after all his years of river travel, also took his own life. As I stated, there is no way to measure what those men lost—they lost their lives.

In summary, a lot of valuable land was sacrificed in the Peace River Reservoir, but how does one measure the value of the power it has produced? Better yet, where would we be energy-wise without it? Isn't life a series of trade-offs?

HUMOUR

We have all heard of cheap people, but the tightest I ever heard of was described to me by an old retired Mounted Policeman. He claimed he knew a man who squeezed every nickel so hard that the beavers actually crapped on his fingers.

~

A trapper rushed into a doctor's office with an accidental gunshot wound to his shoulder and asked for medical assistance. When the doctor went to administer a shot for pain control the man refused, stating that it wasn't needed. He added that he had experienced two things in his life that were so painful that nothing else has ever bothered him.

The doctor removed the bullet and then told the trapper that he had never met anyone who could stand so much pain without flinching. He inquired what had happened in the past that was so painful.

The trapper recalled how he had been bothered by a bear at his remote cabin to the point where he set a bear trap right in front of the cabin door. As usual, he tied the trap to a toggle log that the bear could drag without tearing free of the trap. One night nature called and he had to go number two in a hurry. He rushed out the cabin door only to find about a foot of fresh snow. In a panic, he dropped his drawers and let fly, only to have the load land right on the tongue of the bear trap. It jumped up and grabbed him by the privates and the trapper said that it was the worst pain he had ever known.

The doctor thought about it for a minute and then asked, "You said you had known terrible pain twice, what was the other time?"

The trapper grimaced as he remembered, "Oh! That's when I hit the end of the chain!"

~

A farmer named Luke was out working his fields when he noticed a neighbouring farmer named Zeke driving by with his team of horses. Rumour had it that, although being a recluse, Zeke was quite knowledgeable about the care of horses. Also well-known throughout the area was the fact that Zeke was a man of few words. Luke hurried himself out to the road and shouted, "Zeke, hold up there for a minute."

Zeke shouted out in his roaring voice, "Whoa, whoa." (Which in horse language means stop.)

Luke implored, "Say there Zeke, one of my horses has the colic. What did you give your horse when he had the colic?"

Instantly Zeke replied, "Turpentine, giddap." (Which in horse language means get going).

Two weeks later Luke was back in his fields when he spotted Zeke approaching. Again he hurried out to the road and shouted, "Hey there Zeke, hold up a minute."

Again Zeke roared out. "Whoa, whoa there."

"Say there Zeke, I gave my horse turpentine like you said and it killed him."

Back came Zeke's response, "Killed mine too, giddap."

As stated, Zeke was a man of few words.

~

One of my coffee buddies told me the following story and swears that it actually took place. A policeman was on patrol many years ago when he spotted a driver who aroused his curiosity. He pulled the male driver over and was checking his license and insurance papers when the man in the back seat started muttering something. For some reason this gentleman had taken a keen interest in the policeman's spurs, which of course were attached to his boots.

At the same time the man would take the odd pull from a half bottle of whisky that he held between his legs. Suddenly he muttered, "Twinkle, twinkle, little spur; I wonder what the hell you're fer!"

Instantly the policeman grabbed the half bottle of whisky, threw it out the window to the edge of the road and then destroyed it with one well-placed kick from one of his spurs. Then he stuck his head in the window of the car and shouted, "Twinkle, twinkle, little spur; now you know what the hell they're fer!"

~

A typical Texan was visiting a fellow rancher in Australia and was in the process of touring the man's ranch. He asked, "How much land do you have on this spread?"

The Aussie replied, "Oh! I guess about fifty acres."

The Texan replied, "Well, I guess that's a nice little stump farm."

Back came the Aussie with, "And how much land do you have in Texas?"

"A little over fifty thousand acres," came the reply.

And so it went, everything the Aussie said was put down until he finally quit talking.

Luck came his way that afternoon when a kangaroo hopped across the road in front of their vehicle. This led the Texan to exclaim, "What the hell was that?"

Instantly the Aussie tried to get revenge by answering in a condescending voice, "What, haven't you got field mice in Texas?"

Once again the Texan outwitted him by saying, "Well sure, but I guess I never seen a baby one before."

~

Here is one of the many stories that made its way off the Fraser River that is worth remembering in my opinion. It seems that several trappers were partying in Dome Creek for several days when they noticed something very strange. The table was covered with about a thousand mosquitoes. They were lying on their backs with their feet up in the air, bouncing this way and that, unable to fly. The men finally solved the mystery when they realized that the mosquitoes were drunk. They had been feeding on the blood of these party-goers and were all drunk out of their minds. After that whenever those men were going to have a party one of them would say, "We're going to bring three bottles, two for us and one for the mosquitoes."

~

Perhaps the biggest exaggeration I ever heard came from some of the pioneers in Dome Creek when they defined their method of determining if they had been to a great party. If there were footprints all over the ceiling it indicated that the party had been a roaring success. I've heard of people getting high before, but not quite that high. When referring to love, these men used to say that love is blind, but it all equaled out, because marriage is a great eye-opener.

~

Most people in the Prince George area will remember Bob Harkins who served the community for many years as a radio commentator and TV host. For a time, he and his wife, Barbara, stayed at Nina Creek in the Manson Creek area. One of his favourite tales concerned a store owner in that area who had a strange method of dealing with his customers. The owner was busy in the back room of the store stocking shelves and had hired a woman to run the till. One day a woman entered the store and approached the counter with some goods she wanted to purchase. One item was a can of jam and as the woman at the till didn't know the price she shouted, "How much do you charge for the large cans of strawberry jam?"

Instantly the answer came back, "Who is it for?"

Different prices for different folks.

~

Bob had another story from the Manson Creek area that is worth keeping. One cold, winter morning he went to the outdoor biffy to obey nature's calling. As he sat blissfully unaware, a set of claws raked down his jewels. Bob claimed that he came out the toilet door with his pants down around his knees. Turns out, it was their cat that had been hiding down the hole until a swinging object aroused its curiosity. From that day on, Bob always checked the lower part of the biffy before seating himself.

~

Fishermens' stories should be taken at face value; by that I mean that they would not exaggerate. My friend Ed is an example. So when he told me a fish story about the Chilcotin, I had no choice but to believe him. It seems he was walking along a stream one day when he made an astounding discovery. The stream, which measured about one metre across, had such an abundance of fish that it had to be seen to be believed. Not only that, but they were so huge that when they wanted to change direction they had to jump up in the air and make a U-turn. They were so large that they could not turn around in the stream. I am sorry to state that he neglected to get any pictures of these fish.

~

One of my favourite sayings came from trapper/guide Hap Bowden of Quesnel. He always delivered it as a toast, "Here's to the very best years of my life, tucked in the arms of another man's wife—my mother's.

~

During my years with the British Columbia Forest Service, I attended a great number of wildfires and, consequently, I met a number of varied and interesting people. Without a doubt, the most memorable was a Native known as Charlie. He was one of eight Native firefighters who came by helicopter to a forest fire I had located after a brisk walk through the forest.

Several years earlier, I had been advised by an elderly forest ranger not to pick a crew-foreman from a group of Natives; the reason being that if I picked the wrong person, that I wouldn't get a lick of work out of any of them. You know, the old pecking order thing. Anyway, I acted on his advice, approached the men and asked, "Which one of you fellows is the foreman?"

Instantly several of the men pointed to a raw-boned gentleman with piercing eyes and a captivating smile. I introduced myself and asked his name. His response puzzled me.

"They call me many names: sometimes One-time Charlie, sometimes Tricky Charlie, and sometimes Come Back Alone Charlie."

I took an instant liking to this strange individual who never referred to himself as I, but only as Charlie. He was the type of fellow who always had a twinkle in his eye, as if he knew something that no one else knew.

That evening at our tent-camp on the bank of a stream adjacent to the fire, we ate our evening meal and eventually the talk turned to fishing. Charlie told us that he knew of a lake with huge rainbow trout that was the best ice-fishing lake ever, with fish that were "ten to twenty pounds, maybe!"

Being an ice-fishing addict, I asked the name of the lake and he replied, "Lake called many names: sometimes Soft Spot Lake, sometimes Tricky Charlie Lake and sometimes Hot Spring Lake."

I asked directions to the lake, but Charlie made it clear that I could only go to the lake with him because it was on reserve land. After a bit of coaxing, he agreed to take me along the following winter. I suggested that it wasn't easy to find a good ice-fishing lake and Charlie concurred, adding, "It used to be good fishing all over before the white man came."

Realizing that this was a sensitive issue with him, I asked, "When you think about these things, how do you deal with it?"

Charlie flashed his million-dollar smile and said, "Go ice-fishing!"

The next day I walked through our fire-camp just at noon and found Charlie leaving camp, heading back to the fire. He had made a small campfire and brewed some coffee, which he was taking back to his crew. I called him back and said, "Charlie, you know better than this; you can't leave camp without putting the fire out first."

I thought I may have hurt his feelings, but he just smiled and said, "You're right, Jack, we go ice-fishing."

During our last day on the fire, I told Charlie that in return for him taking me to his lake, I would reciprocate by taking him to a secret lake I knew of. "No!" came his instant response, "Charlie never fishes anywhere else, Bones Lake is best."

I left it at that.

It was late the following winter before I met Charlie again. His eyes lit up as he flashed his disarming smile and shouted, "Jack, you forgot to come ice-fishing!"

I assured him that I had not forgotten and that I was still very much interested. "That's good," he added, "you come to reserve tomorrow and we go to Squawfish Eat White Man Lake."

Charlie may have thought that I missed the significance of his statement, but I didn't. I stopped him in his tracks by saying, "Charlie, wait, I understand that the word squaw is a derogatory term; what say we change the name squawfish to First Nation fish?"

Back came his answer, "That's a good idea, Jack, we talk about it tomorrow."

Early the next morning we arrived at the lake where we built a campfire, made coffee, and then decided to try fishing. Charlie put his ear to the ice right at the edge of the lake and told me to go out and drill a hole. "Do you think the ice is strong enough?" I queried.

He gave me a pained look and muttered, "Ice always cracks before it breaks; Charlie will listen and if ice cracks, Charlie will holler."

That made sense so I walked out about ten paces from shore and had just starting to drill when the ice gave away and I found myself over my head in the ice-cold water. As my head broke the surface, I heard Charlie's voice, "Check ice; Charlie will go for help."

Breaking ice with my elbows, I headed for shore, knowing that my salvation lay in the campfire that we had so thoughtfully prepared. But as I dragged myself out on the shore, I glanced up to see Charlie burying the campfire with snow. I shouted, "No! No! Charlie, don't put the fire out!"

As he ran off along the path, his voice trailed back to me, "You forget Jack, you told Charlie to never go away and leave a fire going in the woods, remember?" (That's another thing I like about Charlie, you tell him something once and you never have to repeat it.)

I rolled around in the snow for a time and managed to get rid of the excess water in my clothing, and then I headed back along the trail to my vehicle, which was parked about a kilometre away. Staggering and stumbling along, I managed to reach the vehicle and then drove home, where it took several hours to get some degree of warmth back into my frigid body.

About one week later after several days of thirty below weather, I was delighted to get a phone call from Charlie. He told me to join him in another trip to Surprise Lake and I agreed to be there the next morning.

Back at the lake, I checked the ice and found it was safe. Then I noticed a big spruce tree that leaned out over the lake had been cut almost completely off. Charlie suggested that beavers had made the cut, but I thought the cut looked much too smooth. Then Charlie pointed to a large X that had been painted on the ice and told me it was the best place to fish. I took my ice auger and began drilling a hole, all the while thinking what a nice fellow he was to mark the best spot for me.

I finished drilling the hole, then stretched out on the ice and looked down into the clear water. At once I was shocked to see a large pile of human bones on the lake bottom. But an even bigger surprise awaited me when I noticed the huge size of the trout. I shouted to Charlie, "How come these fish are so big?"

"Charlie feeds them lots," was the reply.

As soon as my line entered the water, a big fish hit and I gave a mighty tug. Then it took off, peeling the line off my reel at an unbelievable rate. Just before I ran out of line I heard the sound of chopping and turned to see Charlie cutting the holding wood on the undercut tree. "Charlie," I yelled, "what are you doing?"

"Getting firewood," he yelled back at me. Then I heard the sounds of breaking wood and looked up to see the tree coming down right on top of me. Badly injured, it took me the rest of the day to get back to my vehicle and on to the hospital.

I don't remember much after that until last week when Charlie dropped in to my hospital room to visit. He told me to hurry up and get well because he wants to take me back to Graveyard Lake to feed the fish. What a guy; after all the trouble I've caused him he still wants to take me ice-fishing again. I can hardly wait. I am bound and determined to bring home one of those big trout.

MOUNTAINS

People who have spent many years in the mountains just never seem to get them out of their minds. There are memories, certain odors, and stunning sights that never let go. The sounds of wild geese high overhead on their endless migration cycles act as alarm clocks, telling us that summer and winter are approaching. Many times I have camped beneath the skies when the stars gave off no light. Pitch darkness prevailed and yet high above the mountains geese were travelling; they didn't have a light and they didn't need one.

Communal porcupine dens have always intrigued me. I have seen the signs when the snow melted away, which showed that an animal killed them in their den, and while I have not witnessed these killings, I know others who have. Trapper/guide Arne Jensen of Dome Creek witnessed when a wolverine had dug one out in mid-winter. It won a hard-earned meal in spite of receiving a great number of quills. It stayed with the attack until it was successful. When I suggested to Arne that all those quills must have made it miserable, he replied, "I don't think it makes any difference because they're miserable anyway."

I have had a few requests from people to show a diagram or picture of a bug or bush light as they were often called. Back when flashlight batteries and bulbs were hard to come by, trappers knew they couldn't rely on them, so they devised their own light by putting a candle in a can. Aside from getting blown out by a gust of wind, they were virtually foolproof. My father used them on the trapline and described them as dependable. One just had to re-member to keep pushing the candles up as they burned away. The two-candle light gives off a surprising amount of heat and light, but I would advise people to keep the candles at least three or four inches apart so they do not generate too much heat and thereby burn too fast. If a person puts half of the same sized can upside down on top of the can holding the candle, it acts as a heat retainer and keeps your hand toasty warm.

While I am discussing mountains, I must tackle something that most people shy away from: the existence of Bigfoot or Sasquatch as they are commonly known. In the Himalayas they are referred to as yeti. In my view, some myths refuse to die and it appears certain that Bigfoot is one of them. While there are some people who swear they have seen these creatures, to the majority they are little more than a hoax. This has always been my position so imagine my surprise when I learned that someone has taken the liberty to go online inferring that I believe in Bigfoot.

Are there any reputable people involved in these groups? I can't help but wonder. If so, what experiences have they had to justify their beliefs? And why is there never any solid proof? All the videos I have watched just show dark objects in the forest coupled with some odd noises that prove less than nothing. One thing is certain—if a person has a vivid imagination, then nature can throw any number of mysteries their way.

As previously stated, I spent the summer of 1950 working on the railway section crew at Penny. One summer day our four-man crew was sitting beside the railway

Kim and Kelly Boudreau with single and double bug or bush light.

Wilderness splendor. PHOTO JACK BOUDREAU.

track eating lunch when we spotted a large, black, hairy animal standing upright on one of the rails about one kilometre away. It is hard to remember half a century later, but I think it stood motionless for at least five minutes that we were aware of. Then it stepped forward out of sight in the heavy brush growth that was right adjacent to the grade back then. All of us were flabbergasted; we couldn't believe what we had just witnessed. Speaking for myself I admit that I experienced a strange feeling of dealing with the unknown. Although I was unarmed, my boundless curiosity forced me to investigate. I slowly and quietly walked along the grade hoping to get a closer look at the creature. When I arrived at the spot where I guessed the animal had stood, it walked across a little opening in the forest less than twenty metres from me, and I clearly saw that it was a large black bear. For some reason it never occurred to me or the other men that a bear could stand upright stationary on the rail for any length of time, so we had set ourselves up for believing it was some mysterious animal. Looking at it in a different way, I wonder what story we would have brought home if I hadn't checked it out.

If Mr. Sasquatch does exist in the mountains I've travelled, then he must be nocturnal because if he had moved during the hours of daylight we would have seen him during the endless hours and years that we spent glassing with binoculars. Another thing—he must hibernate during the winter months or he would easily have been tracked and brought into the light of day.

Some reports are so ridiculous that I have to take them as humour. Such as the March 12, 2009 report of Sasquatch tracks near Moricetown, BC. Imagine tracks in a metre of snow and an investigator takes some pictures but doesn't follow the tracks. How easy it would be for several people to track it and for the first time prove the existence of Bigfoot. The poor creature would be exposed in a day or two at the most. But I have an easier solution: just backtrack the beast and find out which house it came out of.

So much for our elusive Sasquatch, but what about the abominable snowman or yeti of the Himalayas? Are all the people who claim to have seen them, and their huge footprints in the snow, nothing more than cranks? Could so many experienced mountaineers be fooled and not be able to recognize human footprints? I refuse to believe that. In fact, the tales about the yetis became so commonplace that the world-famous mountaineer Sir Edmund Hillary led an expedition to the Himalayas in 1960–61 to look for them. One of their priorities was to either prove or disprove the existence of the yeti. The results of this trip were published in the book *High in the Clean Cold Air*. As well, a shortened and in my opinion more interesting version was carried in the October 1962 edition of *National Geographic* magazine.

Ten years prior to their trip, the famous mountaineer Eric Shipton had photographed many human footprints on the Melung Glacier. In total, three separate expeditions had gone to the Himalayas with the express purpose of finding the yeti, but to no avail. For his journey, Hillary chose the Rolwaling and Solu Khumbu area of Nepal.

Armed with Capchur guns (drug-filled hypodermic needles), sporting rifles and shotguns, they were prepared for any eventuality. Hillary's co-author, Desmond Doig, wrote, "In convenient proximity to our selected mountain and glacier were the wild unfrequented valleys of the Rolwaling and Solu Khumbu areas in which the yeti probably lived and the high snow-covered peaks on which it left its footprints."

Their first stay was at the Lake of Milk on the Ripimu Glacier between 4,785 and 5,486 metres (15,700 and 18,000 feet). On

October 15, an unmistakable, undisturbed set of human footprints were found and photographed, judged to be size 15–18, at an elevation of 5,486 metres (18,000 feet). After a thorough examination it was decided that more proof was required before acknowledging that they were yeti tracks. Some of the prints appeared to have toes on the heel and according to Des, "Local legend has the feet of the snowman facing back to front."

Three days later at 7,244 metres (18,400 feet) expedition member Larry Swon found another set of yeti footprints. Sherpa packers confirmed a yeti. On October 18, they found half a mile of perfect footprints. Des Doig noted, "All believed they belonged to the animal that prowled our camp the night before sniffling and snuffling outside our tents and nosing about some discarded sardine cans."

Another move took the expedition to Solu Khumbu through a 19,100-foot pass. In due course, the men came upon two supposed yeti scalps, so after a good deal of bartering with the Nepalese elders and the authorities, a price was established. Des, Hillary and a Sherpa named Chumbi set off on a rushed three-week tour to determine the authenticity of the scalps, along with a dried yeti hand and a yeti rug. They arrived in Chicago on December 11, and left for Paris on December 18. Later in London, Chumbi was to meet the Queen, but because she was unavailable, delegates received his gifts of barley flour, yaks tails, painted scrolls and bricks of tea.

Scientists in all three countries declared the yeti scalps were fakes, made from serow hide. The hand was a human hand and the rug was from a blue bear. In Paris, Professor J. Millot stated, "Nothing serious can be deduced from the footprints in the snow. The experience that I have acquired in the African and Madagascar jungles, where I have followed the tracks of many wild animals, has taught me that, on very soft grounds, very disconcerting deformations are possible and the dimensions of the tracks can be amplified in the most unbelievable manner. On snow this phenomenon is even more accentuated."

An interesting side note is that in January 1961, Queen Elizabeth visited Nepal and asked to meet with Chumbi who had so graciously left gifts for her in London. On their 290-kilometre (180-mile) hike to meet Her Royal Highness, Chumbi's forty-five-year-old wife gave birth on the trail and still managed to keep up with the men. After giving Her Royal Highness the arm of a yeti, which was in fact the leg of a blue bear, Chumbi's wife told the Royal family that they had named their newborn son Philip in honor of the Duke.

Reinhold Messner is considered the greatest mountaineer of all time by many in the trade. He has climbed more of the world's highest mountains than anyone else by far. He was the first to scale Everest without supplemental oxygen, which he accomplished in 1980. He had many close calls and lost his brother on one climb. So what is his opinion of the yeti? He states flat out that it is the blue bear, yet he does not satisfactorily explain the many miles of perfect human footprints that have been photographed high in the mountains.

As for Hillary's expedition, after nine months in the mountains they finally stated that no proof had been found to support the mythical yeti. Perhaps I am out of line when I sense a distinct break in agreement between Desmond and Hillary. Some of the statements made by Des seem to suggest that he felt there was

The author, Jack Boudreau, at Grizzly Bear Mountain.

A pack train in a world of beauty high above the timberline.
COURTESY STAN SIMPSON.

some truth to the yeti legend. Did Hillary take his stand to avoid ridicule? If that was his reasoning I certainly don't blame him. Are there still believers in the yeti in the scientific world? Perhaps this was answered in 2004 when Henry Gee, editor of the prestigious magazine *Nature* suggested that further study was needed before the issue was settled.

I find it impossible to believe that these experienced mountaineers could not separate perfect human footprints that "stretched for half a mile," from bear tracks. There is little if any resemblance between the two. For instance, bears have a front pad that in no way resembles a human foot. They also have claw marks that clearly show in front of the pad, even on hard snow. So what to make of these apparent contradictions?

When one reads the account of the expedition from the pages of *National Geographic* magazine dated October 1962 a different view may be attained. Author Barry Bishop, a member of the expedition, described how they had an unexpected visitor in one of their high camps. He told how a turbaned Nepalese mystic arrived at their camp. A carpenter from a distant village, he said a vision had told him that he would be protected on his eight-day trek to the abode of snow. That night he disappeared from camp.

During the next two days a fierce storm raged up the Mingbo Valley with temperatures dropping to zero. Sherpa wood carriers reported they had seen the mystic wandering in the snow at 17,000-feet. After two unsheltered nights he reappeared, apparently uninjured by the severe cold. Des noted, "Although his hands and feet were swollen and he shivered periodically, any of the rest of us surely would have lost our hands and feet from frostbite. His powers akin, to that of a yogi, also enabled him to munch on glass tubing from our lab with no apparent ill effects. He seemed to regard glass as a delicacy."

This man walked around the high mountains in his bare feet and slept on the snow. Although it took a bit of coaxing, the mystic finally led Barry to the spot where he had spent the two cold nights during the storm. He had just spent the time lying on top of the snow, with the cold storm raging around him. Scientists with the expedition ran a series of tests on this man and found that he was able to control his heart rate and raise and lower his body temperature at will.

Although they made no connection between this man and the yeti footprints, doesn't it follow that it may have been his tracks they found on the high passes? Since I cannot accept that experienced mountaineers are unable to separate human tracks from bear tracks, I have no alternative but to at least suspect that this man and others like him are leaving these tracks in the high passes. Perhaps the age-old mystery of the yetis can be solved right in their local villages. Certainly I will believe this long before I accept that these scientists cannot tell the difference between human and bear tracks.

As for the extra-large footprints, they are easily explained by the sun and wind melting-out and enlarging the tracks. As I have noticed from the many years I travelled the mountains, bear tracks can melt-out until they double their original size and still be recognized as bear tracks.

Unless there is a connection made between the human footprints and these strange men that wander the mountains, it seems apparent that the so-called yeti controversy will be with us for a long time to come.

PIONEER
TYPES

Down through the years, countless adventurers have trodden this spectacular land called British Columbia. Their exploits are often lost in the pages of daily newspapers or forgotten journals. This chapter is an attempt to recall some of the more colourful people who settled the Interior of British Columbia during the first half of the twentieth century. Hardships and sorrow were the norm, but many possessed an intangible mettle and sense of humor that saw them through the toughest trials. One lady proved her worth by being one of the early taxidermists in the Interior. Her name was Josie Haws, and she spent a good portion of her life following her husband Bill along the railroad for which he was employed. Josie was an exceptional person, a kind of jack-of-all-trades, in that she was an accomplished carpenter, as well as a renowned taxidermist. During one interview, I asked her to sum up the hardships that were generally known by her and the people around her. She smiled, as she frequently did, in a relaxed sort of way and said, "Sure, people faced some bad times, but isn't it true that after the worst storms we find the most beautiful rainbows?"

What an inspirational outlook on life.

I recall one of the first times I went to their home in the ghost town of Hutton. Josie had something she wanted to show me and I could tell that it was something she was proud of. A cord hung down from the ceiling and when she tugged on it a folding ladder came out and extended right to the floor. No problem getting access to their attic. This was just one of many things this resourceful woman constructed. She was one of many women who showed the necessary strength and resolve so necessary to face the Depression years and beyond.

~

About 1910, Albert "Fritz" Bertschi left his native Switzerland and travelled to the United States. In 1911 he worked as a taxi driver in Chicago. During that same period of time, his older brother Carl had arrived in Fort George and notified Fritz of the possibilities in this area.

Josie & Bill Haws with Joie, Charlie and Mary, c 1935.

Fritz packed up and arrived by train just as the railroad opened for business in 1914. Because the railroad had just arrived, the trains were having a difficult time trying to stay on the rails. Often they spent more time off the rails than on. The train he had travelled on reached the town of Penny, 120 kilometres (75 miles) east of Fort George, where it was confronted with a slide; just one of countless slides that blocked the grade those first few years. Tired of waiting, Fritz set out walking and arrived here in Fort George three days ahead of his luggage.

On arriving in town, he immediately set about acquiring a quarter section of land, and was surprised to learn that all the best pieces of land were already taken up.

The closest available parcel of land was in the area now known as Shelley, about fifteen kilometres (nine miles) upriver of Fort

Bertschi family picture.

George, so Fritz took his pre-emption out in that spot. To this day, his three sons Albert, Louie and Charlie still reside in the Prince George area.

The main reason I wanted to bring Fritz into this story is because of something that happened to him and his brother during the winter of 1918–19. He often claimed that this was the most memorable experience of his entire life. He and his brother were employed at Hutton Mills, eighty kilometres (fifty miles) east of

Prince George when they awoke one morning to a stunning discovery. Several of their fellow workers were dead in their bunks and the obvious culprit was the Spanish flu. Fritz and Carl grabbed their few possessions and bolted from that camp as if their lives depended on it, which was probably the case. In fact, they were in such a hurry that they left camp without their pay cheques, totally freaked out that they may be next. The ground was frozen so hard that graves could not be dug; consequently the bodies were just piled up in a shed until the weather warmed up.

Fritz and Carl were hired on at Penny Sawmill and later at Giscome Sawmill, where in both cases Fritz was employed by owner Roy Spurr as a steam engineer. Fritz spent years cutting ties for the railroad and several summer seasons working as a steam engineer on the sternwheelers SSBX and SSBC Express, running between Prince George and Soda Creek. He earned good money at that job until about 1920 when the sternwheelers ended their operations on the Upper Fraser River. By 1920, Fritz was married to his sweetheart Emma and had built a house on the homestead. Over the ensuing years he and his sons turned the farm into a productive business operation with sawmills, cattle and a substantial income relative to the times.

Carl was not into farming to the same degree as Fritz so he took his expertise to the coast of BC where he spent years as a faller. Perhaps suspecting that such a dangerous profession would lead to his demise, Carl gave it up and went to work with an excavator. It was about 1950 when his luck ran out, and he was run over and killed by the excavator.

Some of the memories these men carried with them are surprising to say the least, such as the rather odd incident that took place along the Fraser River near Shelley in the 1930s. A fellow named Herman Rothing went to check his setline and found he had a monster fish on his line that required great effort to drag into shore. Imagine his surprise when it broke the surface of the water and turned into a man. A fellow had drowned near Willow River about a week earlier and by a one-in-a-trillion chance, had snagged on his setline.

~

Another old-timer that deserves recognition is Ernie Pinker who became known as a first-class cook in camps throughout the Interior. His real claim to fame was his construction of a road-house on the stage-line to Quesnel. Built at 38 Mile in 1910, it was

capable of housing eighteen people, along with a huge barn that held up to eighteen horses. Prior to the time Ernie and others constructed these road-houses, people were forced to sleep outside be it summer or winter. Imagine women sleeping outside at fifty degrees below zero! Believe it or not, they did.

Ernie's brother Charlie and his wife Anna were farmers just west of Tabor

Roadhouse owner Ernie Pinker, 1948.

Lake. On more than one occasion they were lifesavers to people in trouble in the woods who reached their farm and were treated to hot meals and rides into Prince George. The Pinkers were indicative of the helpful type of people who resided in this area during its infant years.

Since my most important function as a writer is to keep the lives of our pioneers known to the public, I simply have to mention a man named Jack Yargeau. An early-day woods wanderer, he spent several years trapping in some of the more remote areas of this province. In later years he worked for the City of Prince George.

During the winter of 1925-26 he was trapping with Tom Meaney in the headwaters of Herrick Creek, a tributary of the McGregor River about 160 kilometres (100 miles) east of Prince George. During late March the two men were tent-camping in an area several miles from their main cabin.

Twelve years earlier Tom had been assisting Barkerville trapper Frank Kibbee when Frank was attacked and terribly mauled by a large grizzly. Frank had gone to a moose carcass without his rifle and paid a horrific price for it. As hard as it is to believe, Tom did exactly the same thing twelve years later.

One afternoon he left the tent and went to get some meat off the carcass of a moose they had shot about a week earlier. When he didn't return by nightfall Jack strongly suspected that something was seriously wrong. At daylight the next morning he set out following Tom's tracks in the snow and just a short distance from the carcass he came upon the dead, mutilated body of his partner. The sign in the snow was unmistakable; in a quick series of bounding leaps the bear had come upon Tom. We can scarcely imagine the fear that went through Jack as he realized that the bear could have been right beside him. Jack confessed to me that he experienced a feeling unlike anything he had ever known or ever wanted to know. He immediately left the area and realized there was only one thing he could possibly do—he had to get out to a phone and notify the police.

Over several days Jack broke a snowshoe trail through the mountains about 120 kilometres (75

Tom Meanie was killed by a grizzly.
COURTESY CHRIS GLEASON

miles) out to Dome Creek where he notified the authorities. The next day he and Provincial Constable Muirhead snowshoed back to the scene of the attack. This was a 120-kilometre (75-mile) five-day hike during which the north wind was blowing and the campouts at night were bitterly cold. On arriving at the scene it was apparent that no snow had fallen in the interim, leaving the signs of struggle plainly visible on the snow. It was obvious that Tom had put up a valiant fight before surrendering to the bear's wicked attack. Blood signs on the snow showed that Tom had landed at least one blow with his axe. The one solid blow that the bear landed took the top off Tom's head, and brain matter was lying on the snow. Constable Muirhead measured a hind foot of the huge grizzly and found it measured exactly thirty-five centimetres (fourteen inches).

A neighbouring trapper named Martin "Deafy" Dayton got involved in the hunt for the killer bear and the following March the bear was taken and area trappers breathed a sigh of relief. The hide squared out at 9 feet, 5.5 inches, an exceptionally large Interior grizzly. Just who got the bear and by what method has remained a contentious issue with some trappers throughout the years. Some area trappers and old-timers still suggest that it was killed by a deadfall—a heavy log suspended above where the bear would have to stand to get at the bait. When it attempted to move the bait, the log would fall and crush it.

Newspapers of the time gave credit to Deafy for killing the bear and this should not be surprising as Deafy had a multi-year love affair with the media and always managed to keep his name in the news.

When the bear was taken it was apparent that it had been hit with an axe as his bottom jaw was cracked and his teeth spread apart. The bear rug with a full-head mount was displayed in I.B. Guest's store in Prince George for a few years. Although Deafy was offered sixty dollars for the hide, his asking price of seventy-five dollars was not met and he kept the rug at Willow River for many years thereafter.

As to the matter of who really got the bear and by what means, it is impossible to know at this late date. Some people still claim that Jack shot the man-killer. When I interviewed Jack at his home in South Fort George I thought he told me that Deafy shot the bear. Did I misunderstand him? Jack was a soft-spoken man so it

Jack Yargeau with the hide of the grizzly that killed his trapping partner, Tom Meaney, 1927.
COURTESY JOAN WEST

is possible that I erred. On the other hand, why did Deafy have possession of the hide?

Perhaps it doesn't really matter. What is certain is that I have pictures of both men with the hide of this same bear on the McGregor River. I suggest that the credit should go to both of them. It surely demanded a lot of courage to hunt a huge, known man-killer in that remote wilderness area where a serious injury would have meant certain death.

~

During the 1950s a remarkable pilot arrived in the Prince George area. The first years that I knew Bill Harvie he flew a Beaver aircraft and he flew it well. My earliest memory of him was when he flew from McBride to Penny with some Forest Service personnel on board. At McBride a school district representative, in a hurry to get back to Prince George, bummed a ride in the aircraft. This was a mistake, because that afternoon a terrific windstorm hit the Robson Valley. Several of us young lads were having trouble walking along the road in what must have been at least eighty kilometre (fifty mile) gusts of wind. Apparently the airplane was all over the sky on its way to Penny, and as it circled to land on the river, a strong gust of wind turned it completely upside down. Bill righted the craft and bounced along to a successful landing. When the plane reached the riverbank, we stood on the riverbank and watched as three passengers, more dead than alive, were helped out of the craft. I still remember the words spoken by the man from the school district, "Never again; never again!"

Several times through the years I learned just what a terrible feeling it is to get a bad case of airsickness. How I envied people who never experienced it.

Another memory that leaps out at me came from Forest Service patrolman Virgil Brandner, who, along with ranger Carl Rohn, were flying along with Bill right at river level in Dome Creek. As they approached the railway bridge Bill asked, "What will it be, boys, over or under?"

In unison the two men shouted, "Over! Over!"

With nothing to spare Bill brought the aircraft up over the bridge and then proceeded along as if nothing had happened.

George Fleiger of Fort St. James spent a lot of time in the air with Bill. He recalls the day he and Bill were flying along what was probably Narrow Lake southeast of Prince George. They spotted an old tumbled-down cabin beside the lake so they landed the Beaver to take a look. They peered into what was left of the cabin since its roof had caved in and they noticed some large triple fish hooks that had been fashioned from brass and other metals. They didn't bother crawling through the debris inside the cabin and they lived to regret it. About a week later they met a helicopter pilot who showed them something he was proud of. It was a Winchester 73 rifle that he had found a few days earlier in a caved-in cabin. You guessed it; it was the same cabin and pilot John had indeed lucked-out. George says he just had to crawl through a bit of trash and the prize would have been his. As to the owner, it is likely that he drowned or died somehow in that remote area back about 1960. It is certain that he would not have deliberately abandoned that rifle.

Possibly the most memorable of all Bill's flying adventures occurred on Longworth Lookout back in the 1950s. Another Beaver pilot had made a food drop to the lookout and either he dropped from too great a height, or else he misjudged the wind drift, because the drop went awry and some grizzly bears ended up with the food supplies among one of the many nearby cliffs and canyons.

A few days later Bill made another food drop and the look-out man, John Flotten, had trouble getting out the lookout door because the drop was jammed against it. Along with his favourite drop men—the Marynovich brothers—Bill earned the reputation that he could make a parachute drop and clean your chimney at the same time.

There is little doubt that Bill would go to any lengths to put on a good show; such as happened the day at Lac le Jeune when his family had gathered for an outing. Bill had been slated to take the Beaver aircraft up north so it was equipped with skis, but at the last minute the trip was cancelled, so Bill headed out to the lake to put on a show. He buzzed the people a few times and then decided to water ski with the plane. Somehow Bill misjudged his airspeed and slowed down too much. The result was that the plane slowed up and sank in about one metre (three feet) of water. Understandably the owner was not impressed.

As strange as it may seem, many bush pilots gained enormously from accidents and went on to become truly great pilots. In fact, I know a few personally who have survived accidents and I would not hesitate to fly with them. It seems that the accidents made them become much safer pilots.

In search of new adventure, Bill switched from fixed wing to rotary wing aircraft and in 1961 he experienced a pilot's worst nightmare. He was called to pick up an injured man near the Grand Canyon one hundred kilometres (sixty-two miles) east of Prince George, where a cruiser named Sterla Roe had injured an ankle. Bill picked up Sterla and his partner Ernie Pement, and on a spur-of-the-moment decision, decided to show them the nearby canyon. As they came in low over the bottom end of the upper canyon, they flew into an unmarked cable that spanned the river. There was no chance of escape and so the three men went into the river. All three got out of the helicopter, but Ernie was swept into the lower canyon and drowned. By a strange quirk of fate, Bill latched on to a ten-gallon drum that had slipped off the chopper and he clung to it until he reached shore. Sterla, a powerful swimmer, had no trouble getting to safety even with his injured ankle.

And so, here was Bill as a new helicopter pilot, fresh from a fatal accident, and heading into the terrible 1961 forest fire season. This was when I first began flying with him. He arrived at the Penny ball field and was in the process of landing to pick up some firefighters when a dog ran at his machine in attack mode. Instantly Bill began a game of tag with the dog, swinging the chopper one way and then the other in what was an impressive display of talent. All this and he had just learned to fly rotary wing. When the dog fight was over, we took off with the chopper headed for the forest fire. What a flight that was, because between ground fog and smoke we could not see the mountains. Bill moved along right at treetop level with the little Bell 2G helicopter. It gave me the creeps to say the least, but we finally found the mountain, and then guided by his compass, we followed the ridge up to where a fire-camp was being constructed on the ridge-top. This was just one of many times that I flew with Bill in hazardous conditions; I never dreamed that one day he would lose his nerve and stop flying.

Pilot Grant Luck was at Aiken Lake in the early 1960s when he witnessed a helicopter accident. He was slated for takeoff with a fixed wing airplane but because the area was fogged in, he decided

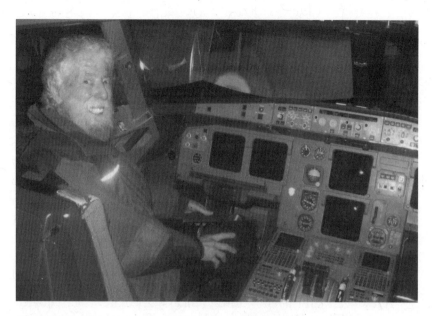

Bill Harvie in the Air Canada flight simulator.

to wait it out. But there was to be no waiting for Bill Harvie, because he saw an opening in the fog directly overhead, so he took
off in a Hiller 12E helicopter and headed straight up. Scarcely a
minute later he came straight back down and hit the ground with
a mighty thump. His rotor blades had iced up to the point where
they lost their lift. Oh, for the life of a bush pilot!

Perhaps Bill's greatest feat with a helicopter was performed in
Sinclair Mills. The damper atop the 30-metre (100-foot) smoke-
stack at the mill was jammed and refused to open and close prop-
erly. What to do? Someone suggested getting a helicopter to hover
right at the top while a millwright hung out the door and attempted
to do the repairs. The problem was finding people to do either job,
because a slip-up of any kind meant certain death for both. Well, I
never found out who did the repairs, but I have it from a man who
was at the scene that Bill Harvie was the pilot and the repair work
was a success.

Bill was renowned for his sense of humour. He was the pilot
who faked puking in a bag and then handing it to his assistant who
promptly ate the stew that had been placed in the bag prior to the
flight. The observers on the plane then all used the real barf bags

and they were not faking it. If Bill knew a person was afraid in the air, he would usually put on a bit of a show for them. That is, unless they were expecting it, and then he would fly like a perfect gentleman. He would go to any lengths to do the unexpected.

The first indication I got that Bill was having trouble with his nerves was when he flew a fellow firefighter and me out of a dangerous spot on Spakwaniko Creek, a tributary to the Herrick Creek. As we lifted off the creek, Bill held the helicopter just above the water and went tearing around bends in the stream as if he had memorized the topography ahead. At any time we could have rounded a bend in that narrow valley and came upon a tree sticking out in our flight path. Finally, he lifted above the trees and I breathed a sigh of relief. At that point Bill told us that he was losing his nerve and may have to give up flying. My immediate thought was that if he flew in a reasonable manner his nerve would probably last for a few more centuries.

A few years later, a fellow forest officer named Steve Marynovich was slated to meet Bill at Wells. Their mission was to lift supplies up to Two Sisters Lookout for work that had to be performed up there. An hour and a half after the appointed time, Bill finally arrived and apologized for being late. He then explained that he had been forced to put the chopper down on a muskeg and go for a long walk because his nerves had really bothered him. His recovery seemed to be complete at the time, as the work went off without a hitch. But that was the signal that problems had arisen and it was just a short time later that Bill hung up his pilot's hat forever. I will always believe that the fatal crash in the Grand Canyon was the main reason for his nerve problems.

Harvie, Captain William Wallace, passed away on March 25, 2009, at the age of seventy-nine. I doubt that many of his peers would challenge me when I state that he was an outstanding pilot in both fixed and rotary wing aircraft. Just as many great pilots before him, Bill came to the Interior when bush pilots were sorely needed and when called on he was always there.

~

Another memorable bush pilot was Ian Watt, who flew the Interior for many years. He flew the Beaver airplanes as if they were an extension of his body. It is my guess that Ian would have died of old age if he had relied on his own ability. During October 1957 Ian and his assistant Steve Marynovich were slated to fly north to Watson Lake but the trip was cancelled because Steve came down with a flu bug. As luck would have it Ian went along with two other pilots and an engineer to Sovereign Lakes, with a pilot named Cooper at the controls. The aircraft they were using was twin-engine Stranraer. Their mission was to pick up the pontoons of a Beaver airplane that had crashed there two years earlier. Later that same day Steve got a call from Ian's wife, who stated that her daughter had heard via the CBC that Ian had had been involved in a crash at Sovereign Lakes. Steve tried to assure her that they were referring to the crash that had occurred there two years earlier. But when she named the others involved Steve had to accept the worst. There had indeed been a terrible accident as stated. Ian was not at the controls that day, but perhaps it would not have mattered, because something went terribly wrong on takeoff. Some people suggested that the pontoon which was attached to the left side of the aircraft may have caused some unusual drag, because all the signs

Ian Watt and passenger Brenda Rockadahl on their way to Fort St. James.
COURTESY STEVE MARYNOVICH

indicated that the plane had swerved hard to the left before it crashed into the trees. No one survived the terrible impact that followed.

Ian's assistant Steve Marynovich went to the crash site and described it as an absolute disaster. Steve flew as drop-man (dropping parachutes with supplies) for Ian over several years and simply could not say enough about his flying ability. That day all the experience and flying skill accumulated through years of service was of no value.

I witnessed a few of the air-drops these men made on forest fires and they were impressive to say the least. The target area was just a small meadow and yet all the chutes were touching each other in the centre of the meadow after the drop.

It has always been my hope that there is a special heaven for bush pilots. Just imagine where our developing country would have been without them. So many people in remote areas were so totally dependent on them. Often they flew in horrid weather conditions, putting their lives on the line for others; lives that were sacrificed in far too many cases.

~

One of the most impressive stories I have ever heard was told to me by Prince George newsman and broadcaster Bob Harkins. It concerned a man who made his living trapping in the wilds of northeastern BC. One day he made his way into Prince George in a state of near-exhaustion. A doctor examined him but could find nothing wrong. The old-timer thought he knew better, so he hurried himself to the Mayo Clinic in Rochester, New York to get their highly respected opinion. A few days passed until the tests were complete, whereupon the doctors informed him that they could not find his problem. Puzzled, they asked him to explain why he thought he was ill. The trapper then told how he had broke trail through half a metre (two feet) of wet snow for about twenty-four kilometres (fifteen miles) to one of his cabins. He further added that he had become so exhausted that it took him several days to recover; something that had never happened to him before. One of the doctors growled back at him. "You damned fool, you just got played out. That walk could have killed a much younger man and here you are at eighty-three wondering why you played out. Get the hell out of here; we have sick people to care for!"

The man returned to Prince George and according to one source, the Game Department insisted he sell his trapline and start acting his age.

~

Bob Harkins had another tale that I thoroughly enjoyed; this one came from the Manson Creek area long ago. Apparently two prospectors were sharing the same cabin when disaster struck. One of the men was frying some bacon and left the fry pan unattended. When he went to grab the handle, it severely burned his hand. He let out a monster yell, dropped the pan, and gave it a mighty kick, which sent it flying out into the yard. Instantly his partner grabbed his rifle off the wall and pumped several shots through the pan; at the same time he shouted, "No pan is going to burn my partner and get away with it!"

Those feelings didn't last long, because one winter evening they were listening to a hockey game when the radio kept fading in and out. In an effort to get better reception, they kept switching back and forth until they had words for each other and came to terms. They set to work and built another cabin, and then moved one of them into it. Next they cut a monstrous wood-pile and placed it between the two cabins so they couldn't see each other. And so that is how they spent the following years—each waiting for the other to come over and apologize; it didn't happen.

~

Some stories told to me by woodsmen just never seem to fade away. One such was the following story told to me in 1976 by a man named Chris Gleason who trapped the McGregor Mountains from 1915 until 1924. When I finished the interview with Chris, he gave me some negatives from pictures he had taken during those years on the trapline. When the pictures were developed I was surprised to find proof of one of Chris's stories. It concerned a grizzly bear he had caught in a leg-hold trap and released because the fur was badly rubbed on one side of the bear which rendered it worthless on the fur market.

My interview with Chris went like this:

"Any other experiences with bears?" I asked.

"Many!" Chris replied. "There was the time—that was in October—when I was walking along the river and I saw this grizzly bear across the river. It was upstream from me so I started walking to get closer for a shot, because we sure needed bear for some food and fat. As I moved quietly along, that bear suddenly waded out into the water and began swimming across. Well, I was sure surprised, so I hid behind some brush and waited. You know, the current brought the bear downriver and it came out on the bank only twenty feet from me. By this time my heart was pounding so much I could hardly steady the gun. Well, I fired a shot, and the bear let out a big 'woof' and jumped into cover. I listened but couldn't hear it running away. I sat still for at least half an hour to give it time to die, and then I slowly moved in, following the blood trail. You know, I only took a few steps and that bear tore out of the thicket straight at me. I guess I just responded on instinct and fired three shots from my .351. One of the bullets hit it low in the neck and it dropped right beside me. I'm telling you I was shaking so much that I had to wait half an hour before I was able to skin it out."

Chris shook his head a few times for emphasis, and then went on. "After that scare, I decided that there had to be a safer way to get bear, so I took my big bear trap with its

Trapper Chris Gleason, c 1920.
COURTESY CHRIS GLEASON

Grizzly in leg-hold trap, c 1920.
COURTESY CHRIS GLEASON

sixteen-inch jaws and set it on the remains of a wolf-killed moose carcass that a grizzly had claimed. A couple days later I went to check the trap and found I had caught a three-year-old grizzly. Right away I noticed that the bear was badly rubbed on one side, so I knew the hide would be worthless on the fur market. I took a few pictures of the bear in the trap, and then decided to try releasing it. The bear was caught by a front pad, so I cut a pole about fifteen feet long, and then tied my knife on the end of it. I slowly worked myself into position and began to cut at the bear's wrist. At first it fussed a little, and then it settled down and didn't move until I was finished. As soon as I saw that the bear was free, I grabbed my rifle but I didn't need it. That bear was so exhausted from fighting the trap that it got up and slowly wandered away into the woods. You know, several times in later years we ran into this bear's tracks with part of one paw missing, and they sure were strange tracks."

Perhaps the reader can understand my surprise to find the bear in the trap picture in among the negatives Chris had given me. I phoned and asked if it was the same bear and Chris assured me that it was. I also must point out that this is the only picture I have ever seen of a bear in a leg-hold trap. I suppose the reason for this was the ban on trapping bears that was legislated in 1926.

People who have found wolf kills with little or nothing eaten may form the opinion that wolves and, at times, cougars kill just for the sport of it. Chris and his fellow trappers viewed it in a different way. During one trip along the Torpy Mountains in September they found sixteen moose and one caribou killed by wolves. In all cases only a little flesh was eaten—usually just their noses, which may have been eaten by other animals. These trappers believed that the wolves were not killing for sport, rather the adults were teaching the young how to hunt—a necessity for their survival.

~

Many people walked before us through this great province and it has always been my hope that we honour them and keep their memories alive. Sometimes I am fortunate and find pictures of these people and consequently feel an obligation to make certain these pictures survive.

"Black Sam" Cadieux and Jimmy White.
COURTESY OF SPENCER BAKER

Author with curater Marl Brown and the 1908 McLaughlin Buick.

One such picture is of a mountain man named "Black Sam" Cadieux (opposite). Sam, along with his 44.40 rifle, was a meat-hunter for the Canadian Pacific Railroad, which meant he was one of many hunters obliged to keep meat on the tables of the gandy-dancers who worked long hours to see the dream of steel completed.

On the right of the picture is Jimmy White, a woodsman made famous in the book *Campfires in the Canadian Rockies* by William T. Hornaday. Jimmy was well-known throughout the Kootenays from 1900 on. He was especially noted for live-trapping mountain goats for transport to other areas.

In the background of this same picture is a McLaughlin Buick which has its own claim to fame. During the summer of 2006 a friend named Steve Marynovich and I drove to Fort Nelson with a plaque made to honour Skook Davidson who pioneered a ranch in the Kechika Valley. The plaque was given to the Heritage Museum in Fort Nelson. While there, we were given a tour of the museum by curator Marl Brown. In among all the artifacts was a 1908 McLaughlin Buick.

A mechanic by trade, Marl got this car operational and brought a bit of fame to the museum last year. To celebrate the car's one hundredth birthday, he and his wife Mavis along with a friend named Bill McLeod, drove it to Whitehorse, Yukon, and returned to Fort Nelson. The distance was over 2,000 kilometres (1,243 miles).

According to the Heritage Museum business manager Bob Laing, the car ran a little rough the first day. They tuned it up a bit the first evening and it purred like a kitten the rest of the trip. A bit of humour was gained when the support vehicles had far more trouble than the Buick. For instance, the van that was used to pull the support trailer lost its transmission the first day and had to be towed home. They also had trouble with the trailer, which must have brought a few smiles to the face of Marl Brown. All told, it was a mission they should truly be proud of.

I admit that I was surprised that the Heritage Museum in Fort Nelson has amassed such an astounding number of artifacts. For the size of the town it can take great pride in what it has achieved. And what a clever idea to put a mechanic in charge—it is obvious at a glance that this man is capable of making things run. The trip to Whitehorse in a one-hundred-year-old vehicle simply says it all.

~

Some memories should never be allowed to die because they speak of such outstanding adventure. Certainly the story of Ole Hansen's narrow escape from a giant grizzly is one of these. His hunter had shot a moose along the McGregor River and Ole had packed the heavy antlers out to the boat where they ate lunch. Both men returned to the moose, but Ole left his rifle at the riverboat, because he had enough to carry with all the meat. As they lifted a quarter of moose onto Ole's back, a mighty roar came from nearby as a huge grizzly attacked. Ole dropped the meat and managed to climb a tree with his hip waders on. His hunter had also climbed and took his rifle up with him. As the bear stood and roared, the hunter emptied all his bullets into the bear's abdomen. Unable to hang on any longer, both men descended the trees and returned to the boat. At the frantic hunters insistence, they returned to camp. The next morning they found the bear dead only a few feet from where it had been shot.

Not one to exaggerate, Ole told me that this bear weighed at least 453 kilograms (1,000 pounds) and when we take a close look at the picture it seems apparent to me that this could be an understatement. I have taken a long, hard look at the 459-kilogram (1,012-pound) grizzly in the airport at Smithers and I am certain Ole's is the bigger bear. If we take Ole's height at six feet minus an inch, we find that this bear has to square-out at about nine feet, five or six inches.

Word spread like wildfire when people got the word about this giant. Within a day trappers from all the adjacent lines had zeroed in on Seebach Creek to get the story first-hand and see the monster for themselves. Also worth noting is that the grizzly is black. Often this is the case with the giant grizzlies.

As for the hunter that shot the bear, we should not wonder that he never returned for another hunt. This was his first experience at hunting and he came within a whisper of being killed.

McGregor River trappers: Jack Shufelt, Bill Yost, "Caribou" John Bergstrom, Martin Framstead, Duncan Barr and Ole Hansen with 454-kilogram (1,000-pound) grizzly bear, 1947.

REMEMBERING
BEDAUX

As a historical buff, I have taken great delight in tracking the pioneers' exploits in this magnificent province called British Columbia. After all these years of searching and reading books galore, I have arrived at the conclusion that the Bedaux Expedition through Northern BC in 1934 ranks among the best we have to offer so far as adventure goes.

During the summer of 1934, an expedition left Edmonton, Alberta, their destination was Telegraph Creek near the Pacific coast of British Columbia. Although much has been written about their ill-fated journey, much more has survived because of journals kept by the people employed for the duration of the trip and its aftermath.

Charles Bedaux was born in Paris, France, in 1886. As a young man he worked as a street hawker luring customers into nightclubs. He was just twenty years of age when he arrived in New York in 1907 along with one million other immigrants. Unable to speak English and with only a dollar in his pocket, he set out to become a millionaire. Described by many as a man far ahead of his time, he went on to prove them right. At the height of his career *Time* magazine stated that if a movie were made of his life, it would have to be toned down to keep it within the realms of possibility.

Charles Bedaux stood only five feet seven inches, and weighed 50 kilograms (110 pounds), so he quickly played out with the heavy labour involved in digging a subway system in New York. Within a month he was searching for new employment. He taught French

Bedaux on left with movie set.
COURTESY ERIC DAVIDSON

for two years and tried several different jobs. Luck turned his way when he hired on as a laboratory assistant in a factory, where he watched an efficiency engineer try to get maximum effort out of his employees. Bedaux came up with a brilliant idea that measured units of work. He talked to the employees and acting on their advice, he approached management with his new "Bedaux Units of Work" as he called them. His methods were an instant success. In some case production went up as high as 300 percent, and all this in a period of three weeks with little or no cost to the company. In a short period of time, his B units were being used at such notable companies as Bethlehem Steel, Eastman Kodak, Gillette, Dupont, Dow Chemical, BF Goodrich as well as General Electric. Soon he had six hundred clients in eighteen countries, in such places as Italy, Germany, England and India. At the height of the Depression, he was one of the top five money-earners in America.

Charles Bedaux often stated that the glory of his life was Fern Lombard whom he married on July 17, 1917. She fit perfectly into his lifestyle. Certainly Bedaux was a master at understanding human behavior. He realized that people were not just buying his products; they were in fact buying him—the man. Many times he hired people expressly to sell him—the man—to top government and industry officials. His vision paid off. One of his greatest accomplishments, as far as mystique goes, was the purchase of the Château de Condé, a three-thousand-acre spread with a castle in France. The expenses were astronomical—eleven tons of furniture and tapestry. Many times he and Fern had three hundred people for lunch. The rich and famous, social elites from all around the world were at their doors. Such people as Errol Flynn, Bing Crosby and all manner of notables played on his golf course or enjoyed endless games such as croquette, tennis, archery, skeet shooting, riding stables and parties that were a nightly occasion.

An amateur explorer, in 1930 Bedaux set out across the Sahara Desert on the first expedition from east to west. The vehicles were equipped with Goodrich tires, of course, as they were one of his clients. Another expedition sent him sailing the South Seas in 1932. The greatest of his adventures, in my opinion, was the attempt to cross Northern BC from Edmonton, Alberta, to Telegraph Creek on the Pacific coast, a distance of 2,400 kilometres (1,491 miles).

Bedaux had been on two previous hunting trips into Alberta and BC in 1926 and again in 1932. On October 1926 the Prince George *Citizen* noted:

Charles E. Bedaux and Rae Rogers of New York, accompanied by their wives, returned last week from the most pretentious big game expedition which has been attempted in Northern British Columbia. After spending about two months in the vicinity of the headwaters of the Findlay the party returned to Vancouver last week with four grizzlies and the legal limit of caribou and goat. The trip was made under the supervision of the McCorkell Brothers of Vanderhoof, and a train of forty animals was required to pack the party from Takla Landing. With two moving picture machines the members of the party secured a number of unique pictures of big game in their natural habitat. The members of the party will be the best advertisers of Northern BC as a hunting ground that the province will have.

Charles Bedaux guiding a Citroen down the hill to Cameron River.
LIBRARY AND ARCHIVES CANADA PA-171637

I ask the reader to remember that Bedaux took this trip through the Takla Lake area. It will make us wonder why he insisted on the Hazleton route to his proposed ranch as we shall see. At the same time, this trip may well have been where the idea for the Champagne Safari trip across Northern BC originated.

In 1934 Bedaux arrived in Jasper, Alberta, and started setting up and training for this amazing adventure. Little was accomplished as far as training, because it was just one party after another.

After much fanfare, the large group left Edmonton, Alberta, on July 6, and reached Fort St. John on July 19 after getting stuck countless times in the prairie gumbo. Clearly, this was a much tougher trip than his Saharan adventure.

The community of Fort St. John was in for many surprises; the Depression had drained the economy, but when Bedaux arrived loaded with money that all changed. For instance, he hired 53 cowboys who were chosen from 3,200 applicants at double the going rate of two dollars per day. He readily paid seventy-five dollars

for horses that were valued at twenty-five. Many horses were purchased or rented until the expedition ended up with 130 horses. A
great many five-gallon cans were manufactured to carry gas for the
Citroen half-track trucks, which were supposed to conquer the BC
wilderness. He spent a fortune and floored the entire area when he
purchased a fur coat for Fern. The price tag was seven thousand
dollars. The icing on the cake was left for their day of departure on
July 6 when Bedaux paid every man, woman, and child the sum of
ten dollars to pose for his movie-filmed departure. The community
was suddenly awash with money.

The main attraction, of course, was the five half-track trucks,
which had been donated by the French auto-manufacturer Citroen.
These vehicles were to meet their match in the prairie gumbo encountered in northeastern BC.

Each vehicle was loaded down with two tons of supplies; far
too much for the rugged country they were faced with. The total
weight of supplies was 20 tons, 190 kilograms (418 pounds) of
which were books. All manner of fancy foods were included, such
as caviar and canned goose liver. One horse carried a great variety of shoes for the fashion-conscious ladies. Last but not least,
was a goodly supply of champagne from where the trip derived its
name—The Champagne Safari. Bedaux wanted to be certain that
his name would be remembered wherever he travelled.

Many notables were taken on this safari, such as his wife Fern,
her maid, Bedaux's mistress Bilonha Chiesa, two geographers—
one of whom was Frank Swannell, made famous in two books
by Jay Sherwood, *Surveying Northern British Columbia* (Caitlin
Press 2004), and *Surveying Central British Columbia* (Royal British Columbia Museum 2009). As well there was an alpine guide, a geologist named John Bocock who was second in command, a Citroen mechanic to take care of the trucks, a gamekeeper and a radio operator, B. McCallum, who sent daily

Bedaux's cowboys.
COURTESY ERIC DAVIDSON

reports to the *New York Times* from where it was carried in the *London Times, Washington Post,* and *Le Monde* in Paris. Also included on the trip was cinematographer Floyd Crosby who went on to film *High Noon*. As a backup to the abundance of film, both Charles and Fern kept journals.

On April 4 four trail-blazers left Fort St. John with a string of pack horses, their objective—cut a trail to Redfern Lake. On April 30 John Bocock followed their trail. He had managed to get the BC Government to kick in six hundred dollars and pay the wages of Swannell and his assistant, along with geographer Ernest Lamarque. They were to cut trail beyond Redfern Lake. John was to play a major part in the decision-making that was needed at every turn on this hazardous journey.

Fern had made it clear to Charles that she felt certain he would not take her into some predicament that he couldn't get her out of. Perhaps with that in mind, Charles had a hydroplane on standby until he and Fern were out of the area.

Choosing the best way was an enormous undertaking because often there was no good choice to make. Rivers and creeks were overflowing their banks due to the endless rainfall endured that summer. For instance, it rained thirty-two of the first thirty-seven days on the trail. The half-tracks repeatedly clogged up and broke down until six weeks into the trip it was decided to do away with the trucks in a filmed disaster. Three of the trucks were run over a steep cliff 90 metres (295 feet) down into the Halfway River. Another truck—the painted lady—was placed on a raft and a package of dynamite was placed onshore and timed to explode as the raft went near it. The dynamite failed to explode and the raft ended up on a sandbar, spurring some romantics to hope that it would eventually end up in the Arctic Ocean. The other truck was left at a nearby ranch. Some sources state that this truck was restored and taken to a museum in Moose Jaw, where it is on display to this day. Other sources say that the truck that hung up on the sandbar was removed by two trappers and eventually taken to the Moose Jaw Museum.

With the trucks out of the picture, Bedaux sent word ahead to the trail-breakers that only a narrow trail was needed, just wide enough to accommodate the pack horses. According to the letters I have perused, some of these trail-breakers were about 200 kilometres

(124 miles) ahead of the main party, so one can readily imagine that it took weeks for messages to be transferred back and forth.

Some of the men involved in this venture were truly outstanding individuals. Bob White, who left the Cypress Hills in southern Saskatchewan in 1928 rode 2,200 kilometres (1,367 miles) to Hudson's Hope, BC. He was one of the lead trail-breakers for Bedaux and left an excellent journal of his adventures.

Just an example of what they had to contend with was recorded by Bedaux's guide Bruce Bocock. In notes preserved at the Jasper Museum and Archives he wrote:

> Amongst the pack stock, we had four mules, and they were the bane of our lives in that mules prefer swimming to fording, and will take off for deep water at every opportunity. This means that you can't pack sugar, salt, or anything perishable on them. Secondly, due to their small feet, they are excellent on rock, but useless in muskeg. Time after time, and day after day, we'd have to unpack them, pull them out of the muskeg, and repack them on solid ground. This wouldn't have been so bad, if it hadn't been for the 'eager beavers' on the outfit, who always wanted us to leave them struggling long enough to set up the cameras, reflectors, smoke pots, etc. and make a real movie set. Finally we had to make a decision between shooting the mules and shooting the cameramen. The mules lost out by a very close margin, but only because they were crippled and couldn't go any further!

From the Halfway River, the party carried on with all of their supplies on the pack horses. This was a doomed experiment, in that the horses suffered terribly from what was deemed hoof rot. In fact, it was later decided that the hair above their hooves was repeatedly pushed up until it caused rawness and infection. As well, the horses never managed to find adequate graze and soon lost the strength so necessary to the demands of the trail. Before they reached Sifton Pass the horses were being shot on a daily basis. Bedaux promised that when the day arrived that they had to kill three horses, then that would be the day they would turn for home. That day soon arrived when they ran into heavy snowdrifts in Sifton Pass, and it was with heavy hearts that the mission was aborted. Some of the surviving horses were sold to Natives in the area, others were turned loose until they could be recaptured at a later date and moved to an area Bedaux had circled on the map. This was to be Bedaux's dream ranch; a place he intended to call the Empire Ranch.

A portion of the trip was successful, in that geographer Ernest Lamarque and his guide William Blackman got through to Telegraph Creek, arriving there in mid-September. They rejoined the expedition on October 3 at Fox Pass on the Upper Finlay River. From there the group turned the horses loose hoping they would wander down to the old Police Meadows near Fort Graham. That did not happen.

Then the entire crew spent five days running down the Finlay and Peace Rivers to Hudson's Hope in six riverboats captained by Del and Don Miller, Bob Fry, Frank "Shorty" Weber, Art van Somers and Carl Davidson. They arrived in Hudson's Hope on October 19, much too close to winter, as they could have become trapped by early snowfalls. Of the 130 horses they started with, only 99 survived to that point.

After unloading all the people, the boats were loaded with a huge supply of oats, which was

Greta Davidson.
COURTESY ERIC DAVIDSON

freighted to Fort Graham, where it was to be distributed to the horses during the winter. Although crew members were kept on during the winter to drive the horses from one range to another, when the spring of 1935 arrived and the horses were rounded up, it was apparent that only thirty-four had survived the winter.

Out of the 53 cowboys and trail hands that had been picked from the 3,200 entrants, Bedaux now picked two men to carry on with his dream of building a ranch somewhere near the Sustut River; the proposed area was to be within a large circle Bedaux had outlined on a map. These two men were chosen because of their abundant knowledge of wood lore as well as their many years of experience running northern rivers. Bob Beattie of Hudson's Hope was reputed to be a bull-of-the-woods kind of guy who had the ability to get things done no matter how tough the going. The other man, Carl Davidson of Prince George, had freighted along the Finlay and Peace Rivers for several years and was renowned for his toughness and ability to traverse the wilderness.

Several years prior to the Bedaux expedition, during late May 1929, Carl Davidson, his wife Greta and two friends, George Myers and a man named Albrickson, left Prince George, drove to Summit Lake and then boated their way downstream to the Finlay River. Then they proceeded up the Finlay to the Fox River. From that point they went through Sifton Pass to the Kechika River where they rented some horses from the famed wilderness rancher Skook Davidson. Their intent had been to go to Rabbit Creek to trap, but the river iced up early and they got trapped at Gataga Forks, where they spent the winter trapping. It was there that a son was born on March 31. Named Sifton after the pass, he was put into a situation of grave peril when Greta got milk fever. Unable to nurse, they considered their options. Seven cans of condensed milk, along with some dried fruit and mush was the only possible food for the baby, but it was enough to get through until mother was able to nurse again. The only medication Greta had during the ordeal was a bottle of brandy, and it was for her exclusive use.

Although it was poor trapping that winter, it was all added experience for Carl. The party arrived back at Summit Lake on July 31, to find their Model-A still waiting where they had parked it fourteen months earlier.

Over the next few years Carl did a lot of freighting along the

Finlay with his lifetime friend George Myers. On one trip upriver to Fort Ware their outboard engine hit an object under water and knocked the motor clean off the boat. They achieved their objective by poling the boat the rest of the way to Fort Ware.

George was always famous for his laughter, and it didn't have to be at someone else's expense. There was the time he and Carl were poling the boat along and George's pole lost its grip on the riverbottom. In an instant George was over the side and out of sight in the flood-swollen river. A couple seconds later he reappeared and the instant his head broke the surface of the water a mighty "haw, haw, haw," echoed along the river. Carl felt that was one of the most special memories of his years along the river—a man that close to death laughing at his own misfortune.

Carl and George had one experience that they never forgot— they had just poled out from a backwater with their boat and motor when they glanced upriver to see an enormous logjam bearing down on them. They had not been running the engine because the water had been too shallow, but now in desperation, they pulled on the starting rope and thankfully it caught and the motor roared to life. Had the motor failed, their boat and their bodies would have been just a grease spot somewhere along the riverbank.

And so, with this varied experience under his belt, it is understandable why Charles Bedaux picked Carl from among so many applicants to fulfill his dream of building a mighty ranch in Northern BC.

Fortunately, for the sake of posterity, Carl Davidson kept the correspondence he maintained with Bedaux. Some letters came from the Bedaux headquarters at the famed Chrysler Building in New York City, while other letters and telegrams came from the castle Château de Condé in France, as well as from the museum in Jasper, Alberta. Geographer Frank Swannell also corresponded with the parties involved in the hope of getting more work with Bedaux. Altogether this represents a lot of information that I have access to.

The mission given to Davidson and Beattie was far more complex than Bedaux could ever have possibly imagined. In anticipation of the venture, Bedaux sent the following letter to Davidson, which he received from the Chrysler Building on December 10, 1934:

My dear Carl Davidson.

Just to have things clearly set down in writing I list below the conditions under which I have employed you.

From October 20th you have been receiving and will continue to receive a salary of ninety dollars per month, payable at the Royal Bank, Prince George. Your food is paid for at date, you will be expected to be settled enough to provide your own food without help from me for one year beginning October 20th. After change in salary.

All the buildings you will put up while employed by me will be my own property, as well as all improvements you will make on the land. To facilitate purchase, if the land is purchased, you will be authorized to make the purchase in your name but after purchase has been affected, you will transfer the title to me.

All the livestock we now have and that we will acquire in the future will also remain our property. If a trapline is purchased, it may be purchased in your name but it will have to be transferred afterwards to me and I will be the owner of all furs you catch.

I am putting these hard conditions down only to remain business-like but you may be sure that if things work out well, I will prove generous enough to give you a happy life and entire satisfaction for yourself and your family.

With best personal wishes, I am,
Chas. Bedaux.

Some of the site specifications Bedaux insisted on were:

• Winter range capable of sustaining one hundred head of stock.
• At least two hundred acres capable of giving good results in cultivation (oats).
• Mineral possibilities within fifty miles.
• Good country for big game hunting (three days pack train).
• Suitability for access through Hazleton.
• Good timber nearby for building.

• Fair trapping through purchase of or sharing an existing line.
• Salmon run nearby.

As well, he listed the following specifications for the lodge site:

• Good view over large, open territory.
• Running good spring or creek, water not spoiled by salmon and susceptible of being piped to house.
• Near a waterfall if possible (for future power).
• Plentiful wood near at hand for fires (could haul one mile).
• Good shelter from hard wind.
• Dry ground.
• Gravel nearby for concrete.

This is just an idea of what was expected of these two men and their three employees: They were to find a suitable site and then construct a passable trail between it and Hazleton, which was to be the only route he and Fern would use to access the ranch. Next they were to build two homes for their own families; build a large ranch house for Charles and Fern; build a large barn and sheds to store all the machinery, as well as clear land and put up many tons of feed for the necessary horses. Along with all the other plans such as moving equipment and supplies from various points, it soon became clear to Carl that it was to be an impossible mission.

Carl Davidson had been hired on by Bedaux as a pre-scout, so he spent part of the winter of 1933–34 travelling through the general area in preparation for the expedition. Then he and Bob Beattie spent the winter of 1934–35 attempting to save the horses that had been turned free. As well, Carl wandered around a huge wilderness area in an attempt to find a suitable spot for the proposed Empire Ranch, which was also referred to as "The Location" by Bedaux.

When he arrived back in Prince George on May 21, Carl received another letter from Bedaux. Two weeks later he sent his response:

> Dear Sir;
> I suppose you will be surprised to find that I am in to
> Prince George so soon, but as circumstances are, I had

come in. The time slips I sent to J. Bocock to settle up with the river crew were not received. As the men were going in expecting to get settled for their work, it was up to me to come in and see what I could do in making some arrangements. I sent a wire to France but received no answer, and that was about all I could do as I haven't enough money to settle with them myself, otherwise I would. I received your letter from New York written April 10 after I came back from the headwaters of the Skeena River two weeks ago. So far I have not been able to see anything of the land in the circle you indicated on the map, except mountains and snow. There is without exaggeration eight to fifteen feet of snow. I could not get any satisfaction from what I saw so my intention is to go up to Fort Graham and take Bob Beattie with me and make a trip in for a month or a month and a half; then see what we can find when the ground begins to show. By that time the snow should be gone if it is going at all, but so far it has been very cold with a late spring. I expect to be in Fort Graham by at least June 10...

Carl went on to explain that he had not seen any meadows capable of supplying much hay inside the area Bedaux had circled on the map. Once again Bedaux should have understood that he had chosen a poor area for farming with an over-abundance of snowfall. The chosen area was five kilometres (three miles) up the Sustut River from Johanson Creek.

During the summer of 1935 the men gathered equipment from all over Northern BC and Alberta. Some equipment was in places such as Edmonton, Prince George, Fort St. John, Fort Graham and other spots. All this equipment along with a mower, rake, disc, harrows and plow was dismantled and taken by horses almost 200 kilometres (124 miles) through the wilderness to the ranch. Out of the surviving horses, fifteen were taken to the ranch area to see how they would survive the following winter.

Countless times Davidson and Beattie were forced to make decisions such as purchasing necessary tools and other items, so

Carl Davidson with his pride and joy: his Pierre Paris boots.
COURTESY ERIC DAVIDSON

they asked permission to set up a line of credit with the Hudson Bay in Fort Graham. Bedaux refused, citing his refusal for them to access the site from that direction. To further worsen relations, a large supply of food that had been stored at Fort Graham simply disappeared and accusations flew hot and heavy. Larry Kempple was in charge of the Hudson Bay Post so he was held responsible and this led to bad feelings between him, Davidson and Beattie.

Since Bedaux was wandering the world it was often impossible to contact him. Several times Carl waited in Prince George or Fort Graham for permission to make purchases or take some necessary action. Their frustration came to the fore in the spring of 1936.

Carl arrived back in Prince George on April 16, 1936, to receive a letter from Bedaux and he responded with the following letter:

Dear Sir,

I arrived in Prince George April 16 from The Location, which is a month earlier than I expected when I left last fall. I have become so disappointed with everything in general that I had to come in and come to some agreement. Beginning last fall I felt so sure that we had the horses well fixed for the winter as we had hay there to help them along with. But the weather was against us from the start when the hay was cut and stacked we had two feet of wet snow, which soon froze solid, causing the hay to mould badly. Such hay as this is unfit for any horse to eat. But this is all we had to give the fifteen head that we got to The Location and the result was that they got colic and died. However the other fifteen head that was left at the Ingenika wintered in good shape as the snow was barely one foot deep. Last year it was the same thing in that area; the snow was too deep. So tell me, what is a man going to do to do the right thing? I can come to only one conclusion, and that is to have barns built to shelter the horses and hay sheds built where hay can be kept without losing it all. If this is not done, there will be heavy losses, grief, and trouble, which makes the task of looking after things very unpleasant. There is plenty of hay there for all horses if it was put up in the proper way at the proper time and put under shelter.

I wish I could picture for you the conditions under which we have to work, as it is hard for a person who has not done this work the year round to understand the hardships and weather conditions in this part of the country. When the rivers are open, which is between May and August or September it takes twenty to thirty days to make a trip to Fort Graham or Ingenika depending largely on the stage of water. It also takes the same number of days between Fort Graham and The Location depending largely on the weather. Last year I made four trips from Prince George to Fort Graham and one trip to Hudson's Hope so you can readily see that it does not leave much time to spare.

We also have had no money to pay for gas and oil (for outboard engines). We also had to hire help for locating and packing and these men have to be paid without delay before there is more trouble. I also bought over two hundred worth of grub that was taken in to feed the men while they were working. As for myself I expect to at least get paid for the gasoline and grub that I bought; I am not asking anything at all for my boat and engine. Last winter I used my own dogs and outfit most of the winter hauling oats to the horses and searching for The Location site.

Carl went on to point out that he had suffered terribly the previous winter by travelling alone by dog team—in one case he had fallen and fractured three ribs. Carl ended the letter by stating that the chosen site had snowfall that was far too deep and the venture was doomed to failure unless another area 129 kilometres (80 miles) distant was chosen.

In response to Bedaux's insistence that they use the route from Hazleton, Carl pointed out that it was a tough trip as there were so

Picture of Carl Davidson.
COURTESY ERIC DAVIDSON

many hills to go up and down. This meant that two weeks were required to traverse the 210-kilometre (130-mile) trip one way. By comparison, Carl pointed out that the easiest way in for both man and beast was to go by Stuart, Trembleur, Takla Lakes and then a portion of the Driftwood River by boat. This water portion of the trip could be covered in a couple days. The rest of the trip to The Location was about 100 kilometres (60 miles) or about a week's travel with horses depending on the state of the trail.

Sometimes many months passed without contact between Carl Davidson, Bob Beattie and Bedaux. This often led to confusion as the men waited for instructions. To further complicate things, inventory such as tools, tents, spare panniers and harness were scattered all over creation, and had to be packed through the mountains. At the same time the men were expected to be building houses, barns, sheds, clearing land, making hay, cutting trail and so much more that is not obvious to a novice. We can but imagine the impossible mission Davidson and Beattie were faced with. At the same time they were restricted in the amount of money they could spend, yet they were expected to take initiative and keep everything moving along.

There appeared to be no end of problems regarding finances, in some instances employees were not paid until many months had passed. In response to a letter from Bedaux inquiring what had been accomplished, written on June 8th, 1935 and received by Carl on September 1st, Carl wrote from Fort Graham:

Dear Sir,

In answer to your question, "What does the $450 to rivermen represent?" I beg to advise that it is the sum required to pay for transportation of the Bedaux Sub-Arctic Expedition from Whitewater, BC, to Hudson Hope, BC. This money should have been received through T. Bocock, agent for the above expedition, but he was transferred elsewhere [Africa] in the meantime. The $564 is to pay for services to men in taking care of the expedition horses, and in locating ground for Mr. Bedaux's hunting base...

And in answer to your second question, "What have you and R. Beattie accomplished for Mr. Bedaux from November 1, 1934 to May 31, 1935? I beg to state that during that period we were engaged in herding the expedition horses from one feeding place to another. If you realize what winter conditions are, here, you will be interested to know that, personally I have travelled an average of twenty-four kilometres (fifteen miles) per day, on foot, pushing or pulling oats for the horses, aided by a dog-team, through snow from six to eight feet deep. The weather temperature varied from zero to minus sixty below.

This was not Mr. Bedaux's orders to me, but I nevertheless undertook this difficult task both as a sign of my interest in Mr. Bedaux's concern and to prevent death and suffering among the horses.

Concerning your third question as to our activities during this summer, I beg to report that in March I started out on an exploration trip to the site of Mr. Bedaux's location. Returning on May 26th, 1935, I was obliged to make a trip to Prince George because of the unpaid accounts. I had another exploration trip in June. After finding a place, we started in packing the outfit and cutting a trail for the expedition from Fort Graham to transport the supplies required to erect buildings and to cut hay for the winter. The task just mentioned requires the additional help of two men (Bob White and Shorty Kierce) as packers and three men (Lou Gerlock,

George Meyers and Don Beattie) to put up the hay; included among these services is the river freighting. I wired Mr. Bedaux informing him that further progress required machinery and money. I have received the machinery, but as yet, I have no word concerning the money.

Conditions were not going well out at the ranch site where the men were threatening to seize the outfit if they were not paid. In some cases Carl took money from his own pocket to buy necessary things, such as food for the men. At one point Lou Gerlock was owed $865 so it is small wonder that trouble was brewing. As for Bedaux, he was so out of touch about what was involved in an undertaking of this size, that in an effort to shame the men to super-human efforts, he wrote a letter to them. In it he stated that experienced woodsmen such as Beattie and Davidson should be able to go far into the wilderness with only some rice, salt and tea, and through their own resourcefulness, build a ranch.

Davidson and Beattie had their efforts continually interrupted by having to check for mail to learn if there had been any change of plans or if they were allowed to purchase supplies. At some point they had to act on their own or shut the venture down, an action that surely would have outraged Bedaux. To give some idea just what distances were involved, from Hudson Hope to Fort Graham was 260 kilometres (165 miles).

During the summer of 1935 Lou Gerlock, George Myers and Ed Bird packed a lot of farm equipment from Fort Grahame to The Location where they and Carl Davidson built a cabin, a cache and put up a good supply of hay. Then Carl and Ed Bird left the area and returned to Prince George. It simply must be noted that Ed Bird was an accomplished river-hog and packer. His name will be remembered in the North, because Ed Bird Lake sits just five kilometres (three miles) southwest of Deserters Canyon.

Upon arriving in Prince George, Carl perused some mail from Bedaux reaffirming that he and Fern would only go to the ranch site by way of Hazleton. Once again he stressed that under no circumstances would he consider going to the ranch site by any other way.

Although I was unable to determine the reason(s) for his refusal, there is one possibility. The Natives who purchased the horses from Bedaux in the Fort Ware area never paid for them. It is possible that Bedaux carried a grudge over this. Certainly in his correspondence with Davidson he made it plain that the money for the horses should have been collected by him and Beattie.

Because of this decision by Bedaux, Carl had no other option but to take his dog team to Hazleton and search for a possible route to The Location. Against his better judgment he had to cover a distance of about 290 kilometres (180 miles) through an ice-bound wilderness.

Carl set out from Hazelton and headed generally northeast. At times he had no idea where he was in that endless wilderness. For instance, after a spell in the woods, he found himself to be at Takla Landing, many days travel from his objective.

The previous winter while searching for a decent ranch site, Carl had come upon a sick priest in a remote Native village. He took the man by dogsled to a place where he was lifted out to medical attention. This was probably where the airplane incident took place that was often referred to by Carl. He had tramped out a snowshoe trail for the airplane and then tied the craft to a tree.

Ed Bird, Eliza and Jack Yargeau with noted riverman Alex Bird, 1969. During the 1930s Ed Bird worked with pack trains in the Cassiar country.
COURTESY JOAN WEAT

When the pilot had the engine at full revolutions, he signaled Carl to cut the rope. The aircraft became airborne before it ran out of tramped trail and managed to clear the trees.

Now destiny had a surprise in store for Carl when he was not only lost, but also low on food and supplies. He had spent six weeks in sub-zero temperature after falling over a steep bank, which resulted in three fractured ribs. He had broken his sunglasses and even with fabricated glasses, he had suffered severe snow blindness. He was past the point of exhaustion when he arrived at a Native village where he intended to seek help. Instead he had to leave in a hurry when about twenty Native dogs took after him and his dog team. Carl coaxed his dogs on for a few more miles before he stopped and made camp. A few minutes later a man with a dog team came rushing after him shouting, "Carl? Are you Carl Davidson?"

It was the same priest who recognized him and now offered help. Carl returned with him to the village where he was given a warm cabin and food for one week, while he recovered his strength. He suspected that he slept for thirty hours straight because he was in a state of extreme exhaustion. Unknown to him, his wife Greta had notified the authorities that her husband was missing and not heard from in seven weeks.

Back on the trail, Carl once again ended up at Takla Landing where he tied in with a group of Natives who were bound for Kichener Lake about eighty kilometres (fifty miles) northwest of his goal. He tagged along with the Natives and eventually made it to The Location.

The communication between Beattie and Davidson was so poor that Beattie waited for Davidson at Hudson's Hope until February 26, 1936. Then he and Bob White left for Fort Graham. Little did they realize that they would cover over 1,287 kilometres (800 miles) before they returned to Hudson's Hope. During their travels along the frozen waterways, they met a man named King Gething who had been travelling by boat. His boat had become frozen in the ice and he had to spend a night out in the boat until the ice set up enough to walk on. He was in serious trouble by morning when he got to shore and warmed up with a roaring fire. This was but one of the dangers faced by these men.

After the two men reached Fort Graham, they left with a dog

team and covered the 225-kilometre (140-mile) stretch to The Location only to find that Davidson had not arrived. Fearing for his safety, they took the two men who had been looking after things at The Location—Lou Gerlock and George Myers—and headed down the Sustut River with two dog teams. They arrived at the Sustut Canyon only to look down three or four hundred feet to see where a dog team and sleigh had turned around and retreated. They felt sure it had to have been Davidson.

They followed the trail to Bear Lake where they learned that Carl had been there and also heard a radio report that Carl's wife had reported her husband missing and not heard from for seven weeks. In one spot along his trail they found where he had blazed his way into a canyon where, because he was alone, he was unable to scale the walls with his dogs and sled. He had been forced to backtrack and go a different way, leaving many miles of trail that could not be utilized.

A few days later they were reunited at the ranch where Carl learned that the hay had all molded and the horses had been dead since before the New Year. Short on food, George and Bob White had dared to eat some old dog salmon that made them violently ill, to the point that they spent a great deal of time leaving footprints in the snow.

Thoroughly disgusted, noting that the snow was deeper than the cabin was high, they all had their fill of the woods. George and Lou had spent months in this leaky cabin without windows and only a tarp hanging down for a door. No wonder they were more than anxious to get out after what they had endured; after Carl had a few days' rest they headed for Takla Lake, 225 kilometres (140 miles) away, and then on to Prince George.

Bob White and Bob Beattie stayed and cut shakes for the buildings that were to be built the following summer, but since they were short of food and the caribou meat had soured, they decided to head for home over Wrede Creek Pass. It was April 18, and the snow was melting when they departed the area for their respective homes in Hudson's Hope. Little did they realize just what a tough trip was in store for them.

The two Bobs made fifteen kilometres (nine miles) the first day and by 11:00 a.m. they had to quit because they were breaking through the snow. They spent three more days in that camp before it froze hard enough to get them going again. At this point they were worried as they were desperately short of food. They spotted a flock of ptarmigan across a steep gulley from their camp but were unable to get to them in the deep, loose snow. One can but imagine their frustration at seeing fresh food so close and not being able to reach it.

They eventually got to a moose Shorty Weber had shot about five weeks earlier, only to find that the wolves had found it and there was nothing but bones left. They took the bones and that evening roasted them over a fire and had a marvelous meal out of the bone marrow.

If ever we feel that we are enduring tough times, we only need compare them to the trip these two men made. Toward the end of their trek, they had run out of grease so the bannock was always burnt. They even ran out of tea and so drank hot water. Sour meat and fish that had gone rancid—even *that* beat snowballs for providing energy. And so the men stoically faced their situation without complaint.

On their journey down toward Fort Graham, they found thirteen horses still alive after their second winter on their own in the woods. Bob White took time out to carry rock salt back to the horses, before they continued on an adventurous return trip to Hudson's Hope.

During the summer of 1936 Bedaux gave permission to hire two men to transport equipment from Fort Graham to The Location by the Sustut River. The freighting was in charge of Bob White and partner Shorty Kierce. Bob later wrote a book about his many adventures in the North. Called *Bannock and Beans*, it was written in longhand which makes it a tough read. But there is good news, because author Jay Sherwood of Langley, BC published this book with the Royal BC Museum in spring 2009. There is a great deal of information to be gleaned from its pages. It gives one a vivid picture of just how hard people worked under horrid conditions about seventy years ago. For instance, they often slept outdoors with inferior sleeping bags, which forced them to stay up most of the long nights to keep a fire going. There were mosquitoes and flies that would not allow sleep unless they had netting to cover their heads. Or they had to ford icy streams when there was snow on the ground, which meant they had to walk with wet feet day after day. Without exaggeration, I have never read a book filled with so much adventure.

These two men spent the entire summer packing through some beautiful mountains, and adventure was their lot every day. One story worth mentioning occurred after they had forded a river with their horses. Snow covered the ground so they were suffering from extreme cold. They found a large tree with many dried branches near the trunk, lit a fire and hung their clothes and boots on adjacent limbs to dry. As they turned this way and that in an effort to keep their naked bodies warm, the fire suddenly raced up the tree, setting all the branches ablaze. Picture these poor men as they took their wet clothes and wet boots out into the snow and got back into them. They were cold before they took them off, so imagine what it was like to put them back on again when they were wet. Surely that was one memory Bob never forgot.

The packing was almost finished by August, when a friendly Native known as Indian Toma approached Bob White and told him that a man was coming through the mountains looking for him. Toma added that he thought the man may have got lost. As it turned out, he was correct and Bob back-trailed until he finally found him. The man turned out to be a former acquaintance of Bob's, a trouble-shooter named Jack McDougall out of Prince George. He informed them that Bedaux was shutting the entire operation down. These men were to take their pack train back to The Location and notify Beattie and the crew that they were finished. Then they were to pack everything of value back to Fort Graham. The machinery such as the mower, rake, plow and disc that had been taken in with such a degree of time and effort was abandoned at The Location.

During one of the packing trips to the ranch, Bob White had met the aforementioned Indian Toma, who had taken a liking to him. Always wandering the mountains of the Sustut country with his wife, Toma surprised Bob with a special offer—he showed a pouch full of gold nuggets and informed Bob that he wanted to be partners and stake the area where he found the gold. Pleased by the offer, Bob had to turn it down because he had promised Bedaux that he would complete the packing.

Word of Toma's gold strike made it around the area and a trap-per named Frank "Shorty" Weber, who had his main cabin thirty-two kilometres (twenty miles) up Wrede Creek from Pelly Creek, spent three months the following year in a futile attempt to find the strike. As things worked out, Bob White was dismissed along with everyone else when his packing job was completed. Did he make the right choice in not going with Toma? Although he never lived to find out, many years later that area became a prosperous gold mine with the construction of the Kemess Creek gold mine. This was right near the area Toma was travelling through with his wife when Bob met him.

Back in Prince George, Carl Davidson had already met with Jack MacDougal. Jack had received two letters from Bedaux, both addressed to Carl Davidson. If Jack felt that Carl had performed well on the job, he was to destroy both letters. If Carl had done his best, he was to give him letter #2, which read:

> My dear Carl Davidson,
> From the reports I get, I realize that you have done your very best in my interests but that another man more accustomed to horses is better indicated.
> In appreciation of the fact that you have done your best, I want to give you plenty of notice, so your services with me will stop on July 31st. Your regular salary will be paid up to that time at your bank. Maybe I will have occasion to give you other work from time to time.
>
> C. Bedaux

If Jack felt that Carl had done a very poor job he was to give him letter #1 which read:

> My dear Carl Davidson,
> The reports I get show me that you are not the man for the job I want done. Your services for me will stop on the 31st of May. I am sorry we had to lose so many horses. I hope you will have better luck on your next job.
>
> C. Bedaux

What really stands out is—just what did Bedaux expect of Jack MacDougal? Since he was Bob Beattie's brother-in-law, he certainly couldn't put any blame on him, consequently Carl's fate was sealed. In Prince George Jack handed letter #1 to Carl Davidson and he was terminated without further pay.

As things turned out, it didn't really matter because they were all given their walking papers. How most of the employees made out financially I do not know, but as far as Carl was concerned when time went by and insufficient compensation was received from Bedaux, he hired A. McBride Young to represent him in court action. The reply letter from Bedaux's representative on August 24, 1939, stated that no more money would be forthcoming. Rather, that charges were to be pursued against Davidson for running debts without proper authorization.

It is apparent that Davidson had an abundance of receipts for wages, food, fuel, tools, boats and motors that were employed during the operation. According to Carl's son Eric, he never was fully reimbursed for his wages and expenses; rather he was out almost a whole year's pay.

When George Myers came out from the ranch-site to Prince George, he wrote a letter to Bedaux dated June, 1936. In it he pointed out his view of who was at fault:

> Dear Sir,
>
> I feel moved to write to you on behalf of Carl Davidson and also about working for him. I was hired here in Prince George September 1, 1935, and by rights was on the payroll until April 25, 1936. I was to help pack and make hay until freeze-up and then return to Prince George for the winter. Davidson had promised that I was to get outside by November 1, 1935. He was in Prince George at this time trying to find out whether he should keep the men and go ahead with building camps, and so while waiting, freeze-up overtook him and I never saw him until March 30, 1936, and the meeting took place at the head of the Sustut River—The Location camp. Why it took him so long to get there I do not know, but he tol me he was laid up for six weeks with broken ribs, and there was some other reasons, but as to them he can say

on his own behalf. But at the time Carl Davidson was in Prince George waiting for information from you in respect to building. Bob Beattie and a helper named Ed Bird were doing the packing, while I and Lou Gerlock were making hay which we did until October 12, 1935. When two feet of snow stopped the hay making, we then started to build a cabin to live in as we were still living in tents.

On November 4, 1935, Bob Beattie packed his last load to the camp. Gerlock and I wanted to get out to Prince George. Bob suggested that we could go and he would stay, but Davidson had asked us to build a good cache to put all the things in so all the mice could not destroy everything. We were afraid that he [Bob] would not build a cache as he was so careless in many ways, and so we said we would build a cache and then we would be ready to go. Bob Beattie said that would be all right; that he would go to Fort Grahame in the meantime and be back in ten days and then we could go. But that was the last we seen of Bob Beattie; he went to Hudson's Hope and never came back until March 24, 1936, just about five months in all. Lou Gerlock and I were then forced to stay as we would not desert the horses, fifteen head in all. We tried hard to save those horses, but the hay got musty with the wet weather. Horses cannot live on musty hay so that is the reason the fifteen head died. We were expecting Davidson all this time, so things went until January 15, 1936. The horses had all died by this time and the grub was running short, and was very poor. All this time we had no light, no windows and no baking oven. I had asked Bob Beattie to bring these things when he was packing and also asked for clothes, but he would bring none of these things, so all in all we didn't have a very pleasant time of it. On January 15 we started for Fort Grahame only to find out on arriving there on the 25th that Davidson had started to come to The Location by way of Hazelton, so we waited at Grahame for him. The radio stated that he had left Prince George December 15. So my partner and I waited for him until March 10, 1936 when we heard by radio that Mrs. Davidson had not heard from her husband for seven weeks. Fearing that he had come to harm, we started out for him and met him as stated. We started right out and reached Prince George on April 25, 1936. In all we had eight months wages coming to us, but because of some mistake Davidson sent in our time for four months. I am not going to try to claim this money but nevertheless it is what we should have. $360 would be the balance.

I am writing mostly that Davidson is not as bad as you think. There are always people knocking other people. There is only one more thing I want to say, Bob Beattie is blaming Davidson for some things that are missing. I know that he is the one at fault for these things. If you care to clear it up when you come this summer, look me up. I only wish to help Davidson where I know he is not at fault.

Looking at the entire debacle in retrospect, it appears that Mr. Bedaux was a dreamer about what could be accomplished by a few men in such a remote area with such deep snowfall. Just the effort involved in finding decent access to the ranch was far beyond his comprehension.

So what led to the decision to abort the project? If the two men in charge were guilty of anything, it may have been their failure to fully point out to Bedaux the obstructions and the amount of labour and time involved in such an enormous undertaking. It should also be noted that Beattie appeared to ignore the repeated statements by Bedaux that he would go to the ranch by way of Hazelton or he would not go at all. Yet at no time did Beattie attempt to assist Davidson in finding and cutting a trail between those two points. I suspect that Bob Beattie saw the foolishness in trying to access the ranch from Hazelton, a distance of about 290 kilometres (180 miles) or more, depending on variations in the route. I believe he just carried on knowing the venture was doomed to failure anyway. As for Carl Davidson's exploration between Hazelton and the

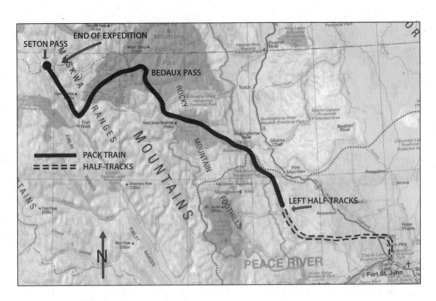

Map of Bedaux's expedition.

ranch site in winter, I think that he embarked on some dangerous trips that could easily have cost him his life.

In the late 1930s Bedaux's empire started falling apart, slowly at first when the unions in Rhode Island accused him of running huge industrial prisons. With the outbreak of war in 1939 he was forced to choose sides. He repeatedly stated, "I look neither to the right nor to the left; I look ahead!"

After a great deal of thought and the endless pressure that was put upon him, he chose Germany. He desperately tried to walk both sides of the war. For instance, when Germany invaded France, Bedaux gave sanctuary to three hundred Americans at his Château de Condé until they could be evacuated. With its 114 rooms, it was perfect to meet all their requirements. This was where the elite of the world met and played together. Actors and actresses, generals and world leaders were constantly rubbing elbows with other people; Jews and German officers were found playing games and drinking with wild abandon, while the world was bogged down in war.

Almost as if it were a river opening up to the sea, the more famous people that came to Condé, the more famous people wanted to come. Bing Crosby, Errol Flynn, the list grew and grew.

Sometimes described as a playground for the rich, its riding stables, shooting ranges, and golf course were in constant use. When King Edward the 8th, abdicated the British throne in 1936, he found a willing haven at Condé, where he and the American heiress Wally Simpson were married. When questioned as to why he and his wife Fern were backing the Royals, Bedaux replied, "My wife and I are still in love with love."

Carl Davidson

As time went by, Bedaux found it increasingly difficult to stay neutral. In 1942 he and Fern were arrested by the SS. Fortunately they had a close friend in General Medicus of the German High Command, who quickly managed their release.

Did the Americans pay him back for his kindness and the risks he took in hiding them? That question was answered in 1942 when the Americans arrested him in North Africa and confined Fern to house arrest at Condé. At his arrest, Bedaux said in his own defense, "Remember 1939." The reference was of course a reminder of how he had gone to bat for them when he hid the three hundred Americans. Instead, the United States charged him with treason and moved him to the US for trial.

On December 5, 1942, Bedaux went to trial in Miami. The outlook was bleak—if convicted he would be hanged; if sent back to France he would be executed as a Nazi collaborator. A few days later he was found dead in his cell; an abundance of pills found in his possession. Did he commit suicide? Nothing definite was ever decided. What was well-known was that Bedaux knew far too much. He had witnessed the collaboration between American businessmen and high-ranking Germans. If he testified in open court heaven only knows how much cover he could have blown. It was better for all that he was silenced.

Looking back at the 1934 expedition, its memory will linger on in Northern BC because many map designations still remind us of their efforts: such as Mt. Bedaux, Bedaux Pass, Fern Lake, Lombard Peak, Survey Peak, Mt. Crosby, to honour the expedition's camera operator, and Swannell River after one of the surveyors, Frank Swannell.

As to the mower and hay rake that had been taken in with horses and abandoned at The Location, in 1944 Skook Davidson and Frank Cooke tore the mower to pieces and packed it in to Skook's Diamond J. Ranch at Terminus Mountain in the Kechika Valley. When seen by visitors about twenty years ago, the rake was still at The Location in Moose Valley, somewhat battered by rust and time.

The Bedaux saga was finally laid to rest in 1974 when Fern passed away at the age of eighty-six in her dream home—the Château de Condé.

RIVER
MEMORIES

Just recently I was studying some old pictures in the archives when a thought struck me. What caused the huge logjam above Tete Jaune about 1911? Since this was no ordinary jam, it is certain that something rather unusual transpired. I recalled that a miscalculation had caused part of a mountain to plug the Fraser River for a time. Sure enough, after a good deal of searching I found that during the winter of 1911–12 a huge powder blast took place at Mile 32

The explosion as seen from the Willow River Hospital.
COURTESY THE EXPLORATION PLACE P995.7.231

on the Grand Trunk Railway grade. This was fifty-two kilometres (thirty-two miles) west of the Alberta/BC boundary. Something had indeed gone terribly wrong, in that instead of a portion of the mountain being blasted away that would have formed the new grade, an entire slab of the mountain slid and blocked the Fraser River for an unknown amount of time.

At about the same time that the mountain slid, a huge logjam appeared thirty-two kilometres (twenty miles) further downriver. For that reason, all the goods and supplies heading downriver for railway construction were loaded on scows below that monstrous jam at Tete Jaune. I have read books about people travelling the upper river prior to 1911 and nowhere did I find any mention of this monster logjam. It appears obvious to me that the two are connected. The mountain that slid blocked the river for a time. The water rose until it forced its way through, taking a lot of trees and other debris downriver to a point where everything jammed up. This caused the largest logjam ever to come to my attention.

Reports from people who encountered that logjam stated that it was about fifteen metres (fifty feet) high and stretched right across the river. In my travels along our waterways I have never

The blast at Mile 32 caused the mountain to slide, creating a big hole.
COURTESY THE EXPLORATION PLACE P979.1.109

seen a jam to even compare with that one. I feel absolutely certain that the two events arose from the same cause.

This begs the question of what happened to this enormous jam. The only explanation I have ever heard came from Prince George historian Ted Williams. He suggested that it had been deliberately burnt out during the 1930s. If that were the case, I have never found anything in print to support it, but it certainly makes sense and offers an explanation where none existed before. What surprises me is that the railway builders didn't try to burn it out during construction of the railway.

Many strange events took place during railway construction. One such event was the enormous blast that was set off three kilometres (two miles) west of Willow River. During the month of September, 1913, a total of three hundred tons of explosives were set off under a sheer cliff that stretched down to river level. This site was one of the original supply points and caches for the railway, which was known as Point-of-Rock.

This was a tremendous explosion with fantastic results, because when the smoke and dust settled, there was the new grade. The cost when converted to present-day dollars was almost five million

The Fraser River blocked by the slide. Note the man standing on the ice.
COURTESY THE EXPLORATION PLACE P979.1.59

Rock Cut Willow River 1913

The new grade after the explosion.
COURTESY THE EXPLORATION PLACE P995.7.77

dollars and there were other costs; in that several lives were lost in all the preparation work tunneling under the cliff.

People came from many places and gathered to watch this much-advertised event. A specialist was brought in from the coast and he earned his pay with a perfect blast. Others familiar with powder blasts claimed it was the most perfect performance they had ever witnessed. The incredible amount of broken rock that resulted from the explosion was a windfall, in that it was used as riprap for many miles along the river front to support the new grade. Some of the many people present that day were surprised that there was not a loud roar associated with the explosion; rather it was as if the earth groaned as all the energy went into moving the rock.

~

During that same period of time, 1911–13, a group of men called Canyon Cats took up residence at the Grand Canyon which is located 160 kilometres (99 miles) upriver of Prince George. Their mission was to take scows, rafts, boats and canoes through the turbulent water for other less experienced rivermen. Some of these Cats earned up to one thousand a month during those two years, comparable to about fifty thousand a month today. At the same time men working the railroad grade were earning two dollars per day, so one realizes that these men were certainly an elite group. One such Cat was a man named Jake Smedley, who went on to become a woods foreman for Sinclair Logging Company, stationed at Sinclair Mills, ninety kilometres (fifty-six miles) east of Prince George. Because of his lead-by-example kind of attitude, he became known to his peers as Big Ugly Jake. At that time nicknames in no way implied insult, so according to his peers Jake wore the designation with pride.

Just how much danger there was in their work at the canyon was well illustrated the day four Cats took a scow through the upper canyon only to have one of the sweeps break that were used to control the vessel. The scow swept into Green's Rock where it was totally destroyed and three of the Cats were drowned. The surviving Cat made his way back to the head of the canyon and brought another scow through.

After the work moving scows at the canyon was completed, Jake spent several years running logs through the canyon with a close friend from Dome Creek. This man was Harry Spidell. He and Jake spent many years working along the Upper Fraser River as accomplished rivermen, driving logs through the Grand Canyon.

Harry Spidell was a living miracle, in that he escaped from what should have been a certain death. To my knowledge he was the only person to have gone under the top or upriver side of a logjam in a fast-flowing river and lived to talk about it. By some miracle his body did not get caught in the tangle, but worked its way through and out the bottom end of the logjam. A quick-witted river-hog grabbed him with a pike pole and hauled him into a boat. This story was told to me by a trapper named Harry Weaver who knew and admired Harry Spidell for many years. Louisa Mueller of Sinclair Mills also remembers Harry and includes him among the expert river-hogs of the past.

As for going under logjams, others were not so fortunate, such as Ed Hooker of Dome Creek, who went under the front of a logjam and perished. He was so admired in the area that a substantial reward was offered for the person(s) who found his body. The reward was claimed by Ray Mueller and Hank Ketter when they found his body in the boom at Sinclair Mills. Ed was only about

Jake Smedley and Harry Spidell, c 1925.
COURTESY THE EXPLORATION PLACE P991.1.142

eighteen years of age at the time and was already recognized as an
accomplished woodsman and guide.

Before I leave off the memories of Canyon Cat Jake Smedley, I
must relate a memorable event that took place back in the 1930s.
One of his employees, a rather humorous man named Bud Ganton,
wrote a song about Jake and the gypos who logged by contract. It is
sung to the tune of "Sweet Betsy from Pike."

> Oh come all you people I'll sing you a song
> About the life of the gypo—whose back is so strong
> He's weak in the mind but strong is his thirst
> If liquor is handy he'll get to it first
> Well, they're up in the morning a-cussin' the cook
> They call him gut-robber, belly-buggerer and crook
> Some hotcakes and bacon and maybe a steak
> The gypos are sure of a big bellyache
> Then back to the bunkhouse and roll them a pill
> [cigarette]
> The teamsters don't bother—they've no time to kill
> Some horses to water—some harness to take
> "Hurry up you gypos," shouts Big Ugly Jake

They work hard all day just a-rolling the spruce
No time for smoking—just chewin' some snooze
A short break for dinner—half an hour to take
Hurry up boys we've our fortune to make
They rush in for supper on Saturday night
There's a big dance at Penny and maybe a fight
Hip pockets are loaded and loaded for bear
Look out—for the gypos are out on a tear
Next morning in sorrow they're shaking their heads
Poor Shorty Blanchard looks like he's dead
The beer and the moonshine is terrible stuff
I'm through drinking boys—I've had enough.
The hard working gypos—a good bunch of boys
Plenty of sorrow and darn little joy
They go into town and blow all their steak
Then come back and gypo for Big Ugly Jake.

There is certainly a lot of truth in this song. The hard-working gypos were lucky to get paid for forty percent of the wood they produced; such was the rip-off of the old FBM scale.

Another Canyon Cat was Slim Cowart who still has relatives living in the Prince George area. Just like several of his peers, Slim was a trapper and all-around woodsman that left a legacy for his descendants to be proud of.

According to an old newspaper article I read, Slim Cowart and another Canyon Cat managed to save a drowning horse in the canyon (witnessed by Doris Ferland and family). During the summer of 1913 an entire scow load of horses went down in the huge whirlpool situated in the lower canyon. The poor horses just

Roping and saving a trapped horse in the Grand Canyon.
COURTESY VIOLET BAXTER

Slim Cowart and Clarence Mespaugh after a winter of trapping.
COURTESY THE EXPLORATION PLACE P996.7.2.86

pawed at the steep rock walls until they went under. They did not have the sense to swim downriver to where the banks were not so steep before they attempted to climb out of the river.

The Canyon Cats took turns manning a boat in between the two canyons. When someone got in trouble in the canyons the men in the boat were signaled by a watchman high on the cliffs. Sometimes they managed to effect rescues in the turbulent water.

Some river memories involve sturgeons, which are certainly the kings of the rivers. Among the largest I have ever seen was a monster taken at the mouth of the Bowron River by Joe Conway. I do not know its weight, but I will hazard a guess that it was somewhere between 300 and 500 pounds. At the same time I allow that it is easy to be out a country mile when guessing their weights.

There are word-of-mouth stories of the Native women in Fort St. James catching monster sturgeons at the mouth of the Necoslie River back in the fifties and sixties. Just how big the fish actually were is open to debate. I have heard some people suggest that they have weighed about 500 kilograms (1,100 pounds). This fits

in with the 500 kilogram (1,100 pound) sturgeon caught and released just lately in the US.

There are also stories of people tethering sturgeons and cutting
slices off them as needed. Is this hard to believe? One of the sources
of these stories was Game Inspector Walter Gill, who was well respected for his knowledge and views of wildlife.

I recall a rather unusual story concerning a sturgeon. It happened
back in the early 1950s at the Penny Sawmill. About halfway through
a night shift, a new arrival from Europe, employed to push logs up
the jack-ladder at the mill, came scurrying up into the mill shouting,
"I quit! I quit!" When questioned as to what the problem was he
stated that a shark had surfaced up out of the river right beside him.
Obviously he had seen a sturgeon, but he could not be convinced.
He picked up his cheque and left the community the next day.

The April 7, 1922 edition of the Prince George *Citizen* carried
this brief note:

**Fraser River to be Declared
Open For Sturgeon Fishing**

H.G. Perry, M.L.A., is in receipt of a letter from Hon.
Wm. Sloan, commissioner of fisheries, stating that Hon.
Ernest Lapointe, minister of fisheries, has informed him
that the fishing regulations are to be amended this year to
permit gill-net fishing of sturgeon on the upper waters of
the Fraser River between Prince George and the head of
navigation.

Several people jumped at the chance to commercially sell sturgeons, among them a man named Ed Simonson. Just recently I
had the opportunity to talk with Ed's son, James, who resides in
Vanderhoof, BC. James has great familiarity with sturgeons, because he was raised on them. In reality, they were a near constant
on the family table during the years they lived at Hulett. His father's license allowed him to gill-net sturgeons at the mouth of the
Stuart River and at Hulett, a small community about twenty-four
kilometres (fifteen miles) east of Vanderhoof along the Canadian
National Railway. The original ferry across the Nechako at Hulett
had been moved to Finmore, eleven kilometres (seven miles) down-

Ed Simonson at Hulett with a sturgeon, 1935.
COURTESY ETHEL LARSON

Ed Simonson's sturgeon on an eight-foot table.
COURTESY JAMES SIMONSON

river, so from that time on, Ed used a rowboat to haul passengers back and forth across the river at Hulett. Foremost among his passengers was the daily commute of school children crossing on their way to school.

As a side venture, Ed made money from time to time selling sturgeon to a store in Vanderhoof, as well as a store and restaurant in Prince George. Because of his abundance of spare time, Ed got to study the habits of sturgeon in the clear Nechako River water.

James rather surprised me when he stated that the largest fish his father weighed was 143 kilograms (315 pounds). It was not the largest he caught, but understandably the biggest ones were difficult to weigh. Ed believed that they didn't go much beyond 180 kilograms (400 pounds) in the upper river. This is a far cry from the 500-kilogram (1,100-pound) sturgeons coming out of the Necoslie River in Stuart Lake.

James told me that his dad would sometimes tie up a sturgeon for weeks on end until he had a ready sale for it. In one case he kept one anchored for six weeks and was positive that it gained weight during that time. He also believed that sturgeons travelled in pairs. Ed noticed that, whenever possible, they avoided fast water. For that reason he always set his nets in backwaters. He hand-made his nets, about two by twenty-four metres (eight by eighty feet) in size, and it took an entire winter to construct one. Although they called it gill-netting, the fish were not gill-netted. They simply rolled up in the net and in most cases were still alive, unless the net stopped their gills from functioning.

James recalls the time his dad got three in a net at the same time. On average, he got four or five a year which was all the market could handle. Sometimes they found strange items inside the sturgeon, such as sticks that were sucked in with the many small trout that had been attracted to the head of the fish. As stated, he often spent hours watching them in about ten or twelve feet of water. He felt certain that they exuded some substance that attracted smaller fish, because they would sit motionless until as many as fifteen or twenty small fish would congregate right below their heads, only to be sucked in and devoured.

Ed noticed on many occasions that sturgeon were frightened by any amount of noise. On one set he used a five-gallon gas can as a float for his net. Time went by but he never caught any fish there. One day he was checking the net when he heard the can bang from the temperature changes. Sure enough, he got rid of the can and the noise and returned to catching fish. The favourite bait for setlines along the Nechako River appeared to be squawfish, while along the Fraser River whole chickens were the bait of choice.

I have my own idea about how the sturgeon attract the trout, but I'm not prepared to put any money on it. I suspect that the feelers or sensors that hang below their lower jaws resemble worms to some degree. Possibly they move them around to attract the trout. Surely something that has been around for two hundred million years should have learned a few survival tricks by now. Some sources state that sturgeon have lived well beyond two hundred years.

~

There are so many people that worked the rivers and canyons, people who risked their lives for precious little in the way of pay. Some of these river-hogs are virtually unknown outside of local areas, such as Arnold Prather who ran river-drives through the Grand Canyon for several years. Arnold spent much of his life in remote areas so the Fraser River was his highway. His one close call with disaster in the canyon was related in my last book so I will not dwell on his adventures; rather I feel that the pictures of these river-men should be retained for posterity. It should be noted that these river-men along the Fraser River generally had poorly designed boats compared to the boats on the northern rivers. Certainly the boats I was familiar with until after 1960 were narrow and unstable.

Arnold's brother, Oliver Prather, was also born in the tiny community of Longworth. He spent at least fifty years travelling the Fraser River. From what he told me during all that time he

Riverman Arnold Prather spent many years plying the Grand Canyon of the Fraser River, 1960.
COURTESY MARG HUMPHREYS

never had a bad scare. At least part of the reason for that outcome was the due diligence he used in all his wilderness adventures. Assuming he may have learned a few tricks I wasn't aware of, I asked him how he managed to keep warm while travelling the river in late fall. Without hesitation he answered, "I didn't!" Truer words were seldom spoken, as it was virtually impossible to keep warm in those open boats with a wind beating at you without letup.

Another qualified river-hog was Eric Klaubauf, who certainly agrees that the boats he used along the Fraser River were narrow, unstable, and packed only a small load. In comparison with the boats at use on the northern rivers, most of these boats were unsafe to put it mildly. In fact, it defies logic that the Worker's Compensation Board allowed their use at all. Eric lost two boats in Slim Creek Rapids and almost lost another in the Grand Canyon. He had many narrow escapes and exciting adventures along the Fraser River.

I remember working with John and Sandy Kinishy on the Fraser River at Upper Fraser during the summer of 1961. The boat we used was narrow with almost straight sides and was totally unsta-

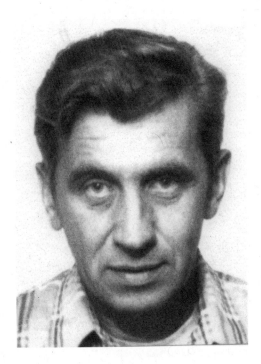

Eric Klaubauf experienced many memorable years of river travel.

ble. It was a miracle that no one drowned in that excuse for a boat. I was more than pleased when that summer's river-drive was finished.

Jim Humphreys of Dome Creek is another man who became familiar with the portion of the Fraser River between Prince George and Rearguard Falls in the upper river. For several years around 1980 he and friends made annual excursions along that stretch of river—memorable adventures for all involved as they had excellent riverboats at that time.

Jim's brother, John Humphreys, was another river-hog who spent years putting out booms and running log-drives along the river. One day he showed me an invention he was working on—a rolling map similar to what the sternwheeler captains used. You could roll off one roll and onto another roll, so you were always reading a map of the particular piece of river you were interested in travelling on. Although John kept his maps at home, the sternwheeler captains kept their maps right at hand. This was a great help because it is almost impossible to memorize 500 kilometres (311 miles) of river, a situation faced by some of the sternwheeler captains. This becomes all the more important when we realize that the silt bars changed from year to year, which forced the maps to be updated on a continuous basis.

John told me about the time he left Cornel Mills with his riverboat and crew. They proceeded upriver about fifteen kilometres (nine miles) to the bottom of the Grand Canyon where a surprise awaited them. The river was in high-water stage and the whirlpool was in an angry mood. It was a seething, boiling monster that stretched entirely across the river. John took one good look at it and then turned the boat around and returned to base. He allowed that it was a frightening sight to behold and said that under no circumstances would he put the lives of the crew in peril attempting to get through that maelstrom.

One of my favourite memories of John occurred when I was working as a boom man at the Penny Sawmill. John obviously had trouble with his outboard motor because he drifted down to the Penny boom where he tied up his boat. Then with the crew staring in disbelief, he took the twenty-two horse Johnson motor off the back of the boat and carried it on his shoulder across all the logs in the boom to the riverbank. This was well over forty-five kilograms (one hundred pounds) and yet he packed it across the rolling, bouncing logs as if it were nothing.

John used to delight in telling about the time he had a helper riding in the bow of his riverboat. The man was supposed to be watching for driftwood but instead the steady drone of the engine put him to sleep. John noticed a small limb sticking out into the river and he could not resist the opportunity to swing the boat in just close enough to shore so that the limb just knocked the man's hat off. Instead the man awoke with a start and jumped up and over the side of the boat into the river. John fished him out and received a vicious tongue-lashing in return. I asked if the fellow ever got revenge and John replied, "He sure did. I had to watch him closely or

John Humphreys spent years on the Fraser River.

Ray Mueller and actress during the filming of *The Overlanders.*

he would put pepper in my drinks or things like that."

There is another memory that leaps to my mind. One evening at the Penny store a local logger arrived with a big tractor. This gentleman was noted for being quite skookum, as strength was termed at that time. He was also reputed for being rather fast with his front feet. In an effort to impress the local inhabitants, he was putting on a show by lifting the front end of the tractor about ankle height off the ground. It was a notable feat, as was proved when several men tried and met with failure. Several of us men were standing around talking when Big John arrived on the scene. It took a good deal of coaxing, but he was finally talked into having a go at the lift. He casually walked to the tractor and without the slightest sign of stress, lifted the front wheels right up to his chest. The show and tell was over at that point, as the man took his tractor and left. John was indeed a powerful man.

Fellow river-hog Eric Klaubauf described working with John on river-drives and states that sometimes three or four men would be straining at moving a big log without success. But when John would take a reef on it with his peevee, it always moved.

Ray Mueller. That name will always carry great weight along the Fraser River. He even went so far as to take a house through the Grand Canyon. Apparently when the house arrived at the Hansard Bridge about thirty kilometres (nineteen miles) below the canyon they found they only had a matter of inches for clearance as the house sailed safely under the bridge structure.

During the summer of 1966 I helped Ray and his son Don with a river-drive, which meant moving logs through the Grand Canyon. I must admit that I was greatly impressed by the skill level of these two men. They moved about on the logs with the agility of cats, as sure-footed as one could possibly imagine. Familiarity doesn't always breed contempt; in their case I think it just developed a higher level of skill.

One memory that will always stay with me occurred when we moved Ray's boat near the whirlpool, which was lying at rest on that particular occasion. At that time I had not studied the history of the canyon so I asked Ray, "Do you think that a lot of people drowned here during railway construction?"

With a rather wry grin on his face he replied, "You bet; as a

Flood of 1972 at Ray and Louisa Muellers' home.

matter of fact on a clear day you can still see four or five bodies floating around in the eddy."

A river in your backyard can be a two-edged sword. It can be beautiful and peaceful beyond words, or it can also be a deadly enemy. Ray Mueller and his family have learned the hazards of living by a river. In the 1972 flood at Sinclair Mills they had the river come right into their home. And they were by no means the only people to experience the heartbreak associated with floods that year. At Penny about forty kilometres (twenty-five miles) upriver from Muellers, my brother Clarence and I went to visit a neighbouring farmer named Joe Pastor. Much the same as Muellers, Joe and his wife Mary were living in a house totally surrounded by water, when the river breached its bank adjacent to their home by a half metre. We drove the boat right up to their house and tied it to their kitchen door. It was no exaggeration or surprise to note that they were stressed right out. When we entered their home

Wayne Mueller in the Grand Canyon, 1971.

Joe's first comment was, "You see that! We worked for forty years to clear this land and now the river has put driftwood all over the fields again!"

Ray's son, Wayne Mueller, also of Sinclair Mills, still travels the Grand Canyon area. He has travelled it as a guide, trapper and employee of lumber companies. For several years he worked the river from Prince George east toward the upper river. Except for the commercial freighters, I doubt that there are many people who have spent more time on the rivers than Wayne. The riverboat he used during *The Overlanders* movie was of similar design to the boats used on the Finlay River, except it lacked the narrow stern, which is not needed in the wide Fraser River. I noted that it was capable of carrying a large load with stability.

I would like to close this chapter on rivers by going back to my own youth in the Penny area. Quite often, especially on a Friday or Saturday night, we would hear the motors of riverboats as they travelled the waterway in the dead of night heading to dances or parties along the line. Fortunately only a few people drowned during those years. My favourite recollection is that sometimes on a summer evening we would hear the sounds of outboard engines on the Torpy River. The Jim Hooker family from Dome Creek used to guide and trap along that river. Even though they were behind a mountain and about fifteen kilometres (nine miles) distant from us, sometimes late in the evenings we could hear the motors as if they were only a couple kilometres distant. It was a special, lonely sound that always spoke to me of adventure. There is something so memorable about a motor boat on a remote river; especially on a quiet summer evening. I have never tired of that sound.

SPECIAL
PLACES

I have been to many special places during my lifetime, but none more special than the Khutzeymateen Inlet north of Prince Rupert, BC. This estuary is a favourite feeding spot for grizzlies because of the abundance of sedge. The Khutz had to become a protected area because the grizzlies were sitting ducks for hunters arriving in boats. Charlie Russell was instrumental in getting this area protected and I certainly commend him for that.

This area is famous for viewing bears because the bears only have two options—accept the intruders or stop eating and leave. Grizzlies are extremely hungry in late spring and their bodies demand the food, so they often do the latter. I don't have a problem with viewing from boats, as long as the viewers stay in their boats and do not try to approach the bears on land. That is the purpose of the ranger station—to make certain that all visitors sign in and obey the rules, which they do.

Khutzeymateen—literally a long inlet in a steep valley. How well that describes the area. It was September 6 when the BC Parks boat dropped me off at the ranger station, a bit late in the year for viewing bears, but a glorious adventure at any time of the year.

When the sun shines in the narrow, confined inlet it is usually after a storm cell has passed through the area, therefore rainbows are a common sight and I certainly didn't get tired of seeing them. This place has been noted for many years as a grizzly paradise, and because the bears were so vulnerable to hunters, some far-sighted people had it turned into a park. Hunting has been banned in the park and rightfully so, as the hunters used to drift in with the tide and be in among the bears before they could sense the danger. Surely all sportsmen will agree—it is not sport to shoot an animal out beyond the limits of its senses.

For my money, this is the best way to deal with bears that are dependant on a food supply such as coastal sedge or salmon runs. Controlled viewing is allowed, but under no circumstances are the viewers allowed to walk among and harass the bears. Their bodies demand this food, so the only choice they have is leaving or tolerating the intruders.

In such places as Alaska, people force themselves upon the bears and then pretend that man and bears can get along well together. I prefer the procedure in the Khutz where people get pictures without alarming or bothering the bears.

Every summer, guest caretakers spell each other off in watching over the area, and I was elated to take a turn. In my case, I went because the person slated to go in, became ill. Right at the end of

Rainbows are a common sight in the Khutzeymateen Inlet.

tidewater, a floating ranger station lies anchored to the shore. A two-inch pipe brings delicious water down the mountain both for drinking and for running a Pelton wheel, which supplies electrical power to the station.

This two-week stint was one of my greatest adventures. Day after day I watched over what any reasonable person would call paradise and seldom did an hour go by when there wasn't something going on. Salmon were running and the seals were having a feast. Time and again I watched as they grabbed a Coho salmon, took a bite from it, threw it away and dove down to get another. What to some would appear to be a terrible waste, to me was a necessary part of nature. On the bottom of the channel a host of crabs wait for their bounty to arrive. Bald eagles dive down again and again to get the injured salmon that have been released but are so confused that they are easy prey for the birds. Cormorants abound in the estuary and it is common to see twenty or thirty bald eagles in the same tree at the same time.

My favourite pastime was watching the ridges for mountain goats. They are a common sight and at times I had more than a

The floating ranger station is occupied all summer to protect the bears.

dozen in view at the same time. One morning I trained the spotting scope just below the crest of a ridge-top to behold a spectacular sight. A beam of sunlight came through the surrounding clouds and highlighted a large billy goat standing right at the top edge of a sheer cliff. It truly stood out as king of all it surveyed; master of its domain. For the best part of an hour I marvelled at the sight until another bank of clouds rolled in and obscured it.

Another day I was watching goats and an animal, probably a wolf or coyote, went by at full gallop on the ridge right above them. I didn't see if it was chasing something or if something was chasing it, but it sure added an element of interest to the occasion.

Every day I took the BC Parks' Zodiac and went for a tour of the area. It was a bit late in the season, and the bears had generally moved away from the sedge and were along the streams feeding on salmon. During my stay I only saw two grizzlies. One was eating something that I assumed to be a salmon. The other bear was just wandering around aimlessly.

One afternoon I was relaxing in the Zodiac, drifting along with the incoming tide, when I heard a bear start roaring up Larch Creek perhaps a kilometre from my location. It kept up for about twenty minutes and appeared to be moving, as the sound got further away. My imagination went to work and I guessed it to be a territorial dispute. As it was along a stream, it could have been a fight over the best fishing hole.

Another day I was drifting with the tide when a wolf started howling further up the river that flows into the inlet. It sounded as if it were right at the edge of the thick forest, but even with the spotting scope I never got a glimpse of it. I am sure many woodsmen will agree that sometimes wolves are much farther away than their calls would indicate. They certainly are elusive when they try to be.

Tourists absolutely love the area of the inlet. All summer long they are taken into the restricted area where stringent rules apply. No harassing of bears is tolerated, and while I was there I didn't see any problems. The few visitors that arrived that late in the season reported in and their company was appreciated after the best part of two weeks alone.

Greg Palmer's elaborate floating camp was a tourist's delight. With its hot-tub, sauna and even a tugboat, it surely added a

Greg Palmer's boat with its two-hundred horsepower engine was a sight-seer's delight.

touch of colour to the inlet. Several times a week an Otter aircraft brought tourists to their camp and Greg would give them a tour of the outer inlet. They certainly got great enjoyment out of watching the goats that were always in view on the mountaintops when the cloud cover allowed. One evening I got a wonderful surprise when Greg invited me down to their camp. Not only did they treat me to a glass of wine, but also a perfect meal. I reciprocated by leaving two of my books for their collection.

I had a truly marvellous time at the ranger station and the two weeks went by so quickly. If I were ever to get the opportunity to go again I would not hesitate. The only thing I would do differently is take a companion along.

~

I doubt that there is a more special place in this province than the Grand Canyon, 160 kilometres (99 miles) upriver of Prince George. It mystifies me that it has not been opened up to the public. Here is one of our most famous landmarks, with an awesome history, only three kilometres (two miles) off Highway 16, and yet it has not been developed. Unlike Alberta, BC surely does hide its light under a bushel. We repeatedly claim that we want tourists, and yet we do so little to make them welcome. I cannot think of a comparable spot that can be developed so easily, and there it sits, visited by only a handful of people each year. What a perfect spot to develop. It is impossible to damage the place because it is all solid rock, and yet the tourist potential is totally disregarded.

Another similar situation exists where the Willow River crosses Highway 16. Just west of the bridge a road winds into the bush for less than two kilometres (one mile) to a viewpoint of the infamous Willow River Canyon, which claimed eight young lives in 1974. This is another magnificent spot, and yet there is not even a sign on

Laurie and Greg's luxurious floating tour-camp in the Khutzeymateen Inlet.

Hixon Creek Falls.

The Grand Canyon of the Fraser River.

the highway to inform tourists that we do have a few special sights to see here in BC.

South of Prince George about sixty kilometres (thirty-seven miles) sits the community of Hixon. There is no sign to indicate that about five kilometres up Hixon Creek sits a beautiful waterfall only 100 metres (328 feet) from a parking lot. An easy drive above the falls is a view of an area that was monitored back in the 1920s when Rupert Haggen and a large crew of men built miles of flumes to develop water pressure for the operation. So many wonderful sights to see and they are unfortunately all hidden from the eyes of the tourists.

The
Dirty Thirties

During the years of the Great Depression, many people went through perilous times. In an effort to deal with the great number of unemployed workers travelling the highways and riding the rails, the government established relief camps. By and large, it was mostly immigrants that were placed in these camps where they received five dollars a month plus room and board. In return, they were put to work on such ventures as road building. Although I was too young to remember much about those years, many stories survived the span of time. The majority of men in the camps I was familiar with were immigrants from Europe. Many of these men stayed on in Canada after war pulled the world out of what was often referred to as "Hard Times." The bad feelings and despair that was often prevalent in these camps is virtually unknown in today's world, therefore a few memories should be revisited.

The testimony of one such story which survived the years is still displayed on a grave at the Prince George Cemetery. The headstone inscription reads:

To the memory of a Proletarian Con S. Berlinic who died 27 Feb. 1933, a victim of relief camps. This monument has been erected by his comrades as a warning. May 3, 1933.

Berlinic memorial. COURTESY VERN GOGOLIN.

The elderly citizens that I interviewed could not throw much light on the cause of death except to say that he was a victim of non-existent medical care. One gentleman told me it was suspected that he died of a burst appendix. On the brighter side, it should be noted that many of the survivors of these camps went on to become solid citizens when the Depression ended and work opportunities became available. Perhaps it is true that time heals all things.

During the years that the relief camp was in use at Mile 77 (Fraser Subdivision), Ed Chambers was foreman of the relief camp crew. One of the projects devised to keep the men active was constructing a right-of-way for a road through the area. Ed's three children, Bernice, Marie and Jim, along with a lad named Steve Wlasitz, had to walk by the doors of this camp on their way to school in Longworth. This was an eight-kilometre (five-mile) hike each way from their homes in Lindup.

I ask the readers to put themselves in the shoes of these children. During the spring bears were constantly feeding on train-killed moose and only the abundant noise created by the children offered any protection from these animals. As this was prime grizzly country, we can but imagine the fear these children felt every time they passed a moose carcass. During the winter months, moose would gather on the railway and refuse to leave the plowed grade, which would have forced them into the deep snow. This meant that the children were unable to pass. Sometimes an elderly man named Mr. Gray would walk them home to Lindup with a lantern and try to chase the moose off the grade to allow them to pass. Other times, even though it was illegal, the section crews would supply rides on their speeder or motor car as they are often called. The last few years the children made bugs (a candle in a can), which allowed them to see the way home during the early winter darkness.

As if animals were not enough to deal with, the children had to be on constant watch for snow ploughs, that could easily have buried them unless they got well-clear of the grade to let the trains go by. So much worry had to have been inflicted on the parents during those years.

~

People in relief camps were not the only ones to receive little in the way of medical care. My mother gave birth to eight children at home without a doctor in attendance. The best that could be hoped for was a midwife, and my mother often reciprocated by attending to other women giving birth. One of these births was to live on in her memories because it ended in disaster. In 1931 a neighbour woman hemorrhaged and died before a doctor arrived in the community. In that single case the doctor was fall-down drunk when he arrived and was of no help whatsoever. He accused my mother of negligence and threatened her with court action. Finally the policeman, Constable Soles, told the doctor that he was out of line and the matter was dropped. Only recently have I learned that the doctor's name was Trefry. His wife had left him and run off with a butcher, which caused the doctor to fall into a period of drunken despair.

A few years later a turn came in Doctor Trefry's life when he caught a ride to Edmonton with bush pilot Grant McConaghy. In search of a new life the doctor went on to Montreal where he eventually got his life together and resumed his medical practice.

~

Viola Weatherly who now resides in Prince George, recalls some of the good-old-days of the thirties. She was born at Red Rocky Lake along the Crooked River in 1927. As a child she and her younger sister Rose spent endless hours sitting on the ice of the lake catching fish to sate the ravenous appetites of the mink her father farmed. They always suffered from cold while fishing. In fact, she still shivers when she thinks of it. Her father also ran a trapline and on occasion he live-trapped foxes that were fed until their hides were prime and ready for the fur market. Besides trapping, her father purchased fur from Natives in that area so about once a year he came out to civilization to sell furs and purchase supplies. When I asked Viola if they ever fed moose meat to the mink when fish were scarce, she smiled and replied, "Oh no, that would have been illegal!"

When I suggested that life must have been hard she pointed out that they always had a large garden and wild berries seemed to grow in abundance. Viola mentioned a problem faced by all mink ranchers—the importance of silence and of keeping strangers away from the mink, especially when they are rearing young. Any amount of stress will cause them to kill and eat their young. Hence the old saying, "That's enough to make a person eat their young."

Loneliness was a way of life, and since there was not a school anywhere near that area, Viola went without schooling until she was ten years of age when they sold out to Tony Zlot and moved to Giscome. They started another mink farm and the two sisters had a tough new job to contend with—packing muskrat, squirrel and weasel carcasses from area trappers to feed the mink. The alternative was to sit on Eaglet Lake and freeze while trying to catch fish.

One memory will always stay with her—the time they caught a ride to Perry Road with Mr. Garland. The purpose of the trip was to get an old horse and bring him home for mink feed. They walked several miles along Perry Road where they got the horse and started the long walk home. Some time in the wee hours they reached a stump farm where Rose exclaimed that she was exhausted and could not go any further. They knocked on the door of the abode and a young bachelor answered. They explained their situation and the young man fed their horse and then prepared a meal for them. The next morning he fed them breakfast before sending them on their way. It turned out that the young man wasn't as sweet as he appeared, because when he met their father sometime later he presented him with a bill for five dollars. This was a considerable sum of money at that time. As for the distance the young girls walked, it was about thirty kilometres (nineteen miles), and much of the distance had been walked in darkness.

As far as danger was concerned this trip paled in comparison to the time she fell through the ice on Eaglet Lake. Her quick-thinking friends managed to find a pole at lake's edge and got her out to safety.

Viola's husband, Norm Weatherly, related a few stories about game warden Alf Jank who became a legend in the Prince George and Peace River areas. Alf was often referred to as a man who would arrest his own mother without hesitation. Although in fairness one must state that with so many people living in the forests the pressure on wildlife got totally out of hand, so it is understandable that the wardens had to take action at times. As a lad, Norm used to hunt deer and bear around their property and on one occasion he met Alf who asked if he had seen any moose. Norm replied, "Yes!

I saw one, but it looked so much like you that I didn't dare shoot."

As demanding as his job was, Alf did manage a smile at times. In fact, he managed to keep a sense of humour, which seems to indicate that he had a good side too. Norm pointed out that Alf, as well as other wardens and police officers, often turned a blind eye to poachers if they felt the meat was needed and not wasted.

Norm recalled the time Alf arrested a man for shooting a moose out of season. In court the man was sentenced to jail because he could not afford to pay the fine. At that point the man's mother stood up and berated the magistrate with, "The only reason my son shot that moose was because I needed it. He is paying for it and I still need it so I'm asking you to make Mr. Jank return the meat to me." His honor concurred and much to the chagrin of the warden the meat was returned to the mother.

As a child, Norm lived about eight kilometres (five miles) up-river from the mouth of the Willow River. How well he recalls the time back in the thirties when his father Joe shot a moose for desperately needed food. A neighbour reported the incident and the next time his father went to Prince George he was approached by Constable Soles, who told him, "I know you shot a moose and I will be out to your place to check at exactly 11:00 a.m. on Tuesday; I'm telling you that there had better not be any moose around."

Not only did Joe get advance warning, the policeman also told him who had reported him. It seems apparent that these law officers had a lot of feeling and understanding for the plight of these homesteaders.

A similar story was told to me by Vern Gogolin who resided in the College Heights area of Prince George as a lad. When he was around twelve years old, he shot a cow and calf moose, which was much needed by the family. One Sunday his mother invited a neighbour in for dinner and fresh moose was the entrée of the day. As a return favour the man reported the illegal moose to the Game Department. Although it was spring breakup with the roads in terrible condition, Warden Jank walked the twelve kilometres (eight miles) in to their farm where the moose was hanging in a shed, and an abundance of moose hair was strewn all over the yard. In other words, a blind man would have known there was poaching going on. The warden came into the house where the children were doing their homework, had a coffee, talked for a few minutes, and then

Frank Wagner at Slim Lake, 1953.

left without mentioning the moose. Who started the tales about Jank being so hard-hearted? Perhaps many of these stories were started by people who tried to misuse or fool the law officers. Not a good plan in my estimation.

Something that leapt out at me was the manner in which magistrates dealt with poachers, especially for shooting moose out of season. For instance, magistrate George Milburn repeatedly offered them a three-hundred-dollar fine or ten days in jail. Of course most people chose jail because three hundred dollars was an enormous sum of money at that time. When we consider the balance against magistrates in Kamloops who offered fines of five hundred dollars or six months in jail for bootlegging, it appears obvious that mercy was the keyword of the times in Prince George as far as poaching was concerned.

Many young fellows did extremely well financially during the years when squirrel pelts were worth a dollar a piece. When wages were four dollars a day, some of these teenagers earned twenty to forty dollars a day shooting squirrels. On occasion they met wardens out in the woods, but they had become so adept at their trade that they were never caught with the goods. Since they had developed the skill to skin a squirrel in a matter of seconds, their favourite trick was to put the pelts inside their underwear where they were out of sight. The downside of this was that the fleas used to leave the dead squirrels and take up residence on their bodies where they chewed their legs and privates all to hell. The money was good but they sure paid for it in other ways!

I asked one pioneer stump farmer if he had gone through hard times during the Great Depression and he replied, "Hell no! I always had food on the table; but those men who rode the rods, they knew what hard times were all about."

I doubt that truer words were ever spoken. My family knew a man named Frank Wagner who experienced many rough days riding the rods. As a young man in Germany he saw countless signs stating that there was an abundance of work and golden opportunities in Canada. Filled with enthusiasm, he arrived in British Columbia just as the Depression started. He spent several years riding the rods and trying to find something to eat by helping out on farms or splitting firewood to get a meal. Perhaps his most enduring memory concerned a black friend who frequently travelled with him. Many times their trails parted and they lost track of each other, but by asking people in hobo jungles, his pal always managed to find him again and again.

Some good luck finally came Frank's way in southern Alberta when he met a sweet young lady and they quickly became friends. One afternoon she asked Frank if he wanted to come on a picnic with her and of course the answer was yes. As they walked down the roadway out of town with a picnic basket full of food, they heard a shout, "That's him; that's my partner right there."

They both whirled around to behold Frank's pal in the hands of two policemen. Apparently he had got in trouble with the law and didn't want to leave town without his dear friend. As the girl stared in amazement, the police loaded them on a freight train and shipped them out of town. Frank told us that for quite a while he seriously considered doing away with his dear friend.

On a hunting trip one fall Frank regaled my brother Clarence and me with many memories from the Depression years; quite a few of which I dare not relate here. When the Depression finally ended, Frank made himself a promise that he would never be broke again. To the best of my knowledge he always managed to keep that promise.

~

An example of what some people had to contend with was shown one evening when I was about seven years old. My two older brothers and I were returning from a fishing trip along the railroad track just as darkness was setting in, when we saw a campfire burning in the adjacent trees. We walked to the spot to find a hobo sitting beside a campfire drinking a pot of tea. This poor man had virtually nothing in his possession and was hugging the fire in an attempt to escape the millions of mosquitoes that surrounded us. After a day of fishing, we still had a couple sandwiches in our packs so we asked if he would like them. The broad smile that lit up his face gave us the impression that he had just won a super lotto. A scant few seconds later the food had disappeared and we were homeward bound. It was a frequent sight to see these lost souls riding the trains to nowhere; their dejected demeanor openly displaying the despair that seemed to go on without end.

~

My parents used to tell a story about a black man my father brought to our home. Dad met him on the railway tracks and during their conversation the poor fellow told Dad that he had not eaten in many days. Dad suggested that he come to our house where Mom would prepare a meal for him. He heartily accepted and as they neared our home, my two oldest sisters spotted them and cried out to Mom, "A black man has got Dad!"

Just what made them think that *Dad* didn't have the black man I do not know; but what I do know is that the two girls hid under a bed until the gentleman left. Not only had the girls never seen a black man, I don't think they even knew one existed at their young age.

~

Sometimes a writer lucks out and receives pictures seemingly out of the blue. Such is the case with the picture of Hugh Gillis' gravesite on Old Baldy Mountain northeast of Fort St. James. The original grave marker had long since gone to dust when Elmer Micks walked past the site back in the 1930s. Fortunately, he was able to take a photogrpaph because someone had graciously erected another memorial on the spot.

The story of Gillis' suicide has survived the years in the form of a poem written by Earl Buck of Fort St. James. With obvious deep feelings, it describes the events that led to the suicide:

By Earl Buck

Back in the 1870s when Manson trails were new
from the eastern part of Canada came a miner staunch and true.
He settled in on Manson Creek when pay was at its best.
He worked from morn 'till evening and didn't stop to rest.

For two long years he panned the dust to fill his poke with gold
and dreamed each night of his sweetheart, with whom he would grow old.
Now the lure of gold was in his veins; it was hard to leave his claim,
but waiting at home was a maiden fair that would someday bear his name.

To Manson Creek and the properties round, many prospectors went,
but the women at night in the halls so bright, left many without a cent.
But it was different with this lad; he stayed in his cabin at night,
for with a sweetheart waiting to marry him, he didn't think it right.

His partner grew weary of this life, and decided not to stay
Hugh bid his friend a last goodbye and these parting words did say:
"This poke of gold is for my girl, so she can buy a ring.
I'll stay and wash another poke, then come home in the spring."

All winter he tunneled in the bank, he piled his diggings high,
and with the breakup in the spring, his dream was looming high.
He filled his poke and bound it tight, and headed on the trails.
Three hundred miles he had to tramp before he reached the rails.

With Baldy Mountain in his path; he climbed it to the top,
and coming down the southern slope, to eat and rest he stopped.
A pack train coming from the south, with food, supplies and mail
met this miner where he'd camped beside the lonely trail.

He asked them if they had his mail, "Hugh Gillis is my name."
and as they scanned the letters, there was one addressed to same.
He took the letter and read it through; they saw his face go pale.
His eyes turned green with envy; it's a sad and bitter tale.

His partner when he reached their home; this maiden fair did wed.
With gold enough to build a home; they lived his life instead.
Hugh's steps were slow as he gathered stones and put them in a pile.
They all stood round dumbfounded and watched him for a while.

They heard a shot and then they found poor Gillis lying dead,
he couldn't bear to go on home; he took his life instead.
They buried him in that lonely spot; many years have come and gone,
but the memory of that fatal place will always linger on.

Hugh's poke of gold is up there; where he buried it in the ground,
and since that day, though many have searched, it never has been found.

Elmer Micks assures me that there are still old-timers around who believe that the gold was found. Understandably, the person who found it would have to keep quiet about their discovery or else risk having to turn it over to the authorities. I suspect he is right.

Another point of view was offered by a prospector who stated that when Hugh's partner went home after a couple years of prospecting, he took all the gold Hugh had collected to that time with him. This meant that he not only married Hugh's girl, but also bought their house with at least some of Hugh's gold. This puts an entirely different light on the story and makes the suicide a little easier to understand.

In retrospect, I think this is the most touching poem I have ever read. After all the years of hard work that he put into his claims, Hugh was not able to bear facing the people at home. A further thought, is that people in the Fort St. James area will renew the memorial from time to time and keep this most-touching event alive for future generations.

Hugh Gillis' gravesite on Old Baldy Mountain.

~

During the Depression many people made their own wine and homebrew. Some suggested it gave them temporary escape from the despair of being unemployed. Sometimes this white lightning, wine or homebrew as it was called, led to all manner of spectacles and memories. An elderly gentleman named John Szerencsi told me a story of how he and a young buddy took advantage of a wine-maker. This fellow was out cutting hay with a scythe and about every hour he would stop and grab a gallon of his home-made brew that he kept hidden in the bushes. After a couple stiff pulls, he would return to his work. The young lads were struck by inspiration, so they found a little frog, which they inserted into the wine. As the two lads sat hiding, the farmer returned, opened the jug, and exclaimed in a loud voice, "It's a miracle; there's no way around it, it is a miracle!"

This farmer continually told the story about the frog that mysteriously appeared in the wine. He definitely believed that it was a true miracle.

WARD'S
TRAVELLING BAND

For all who have read my book *Wilderness Dreams*, I want to point out that the heroine of the book, Clara Ward, inherited her courage and drive from her parents, Lizzy and Thomas Ward. During the Depression years of the thirties these two people took their family of seven children on a whirlwind trip across Canada, earning their way by playing music. Absent from the trip was their oldest boy Jim, who was in the military at the time. In later years Tom wrote about their adventures, and their story has so intrigued me that I simply have to relate it for posterity.

Something I must mention is Tom's view of raising children, such as his belief that we should never talk baby talk to children because much of what they are taught has to be relearned at a later date. He also believed that one should never strike a child as this teaches them anger and hatred. His motto was simple—teach them right and wrong and then be a living example of what you want them to become.

Following is Tom's story, edited for brevity:

During the Depression years work was scarce, and the Relief Department gave only so many days work for each member of the family. In my case, with a family of ten children, I got forty-seven dollars worth of work each month. This meant eleven days work on the roads each month. This was barely enough money to keep body and soul together, so in 1936 I decided to teach my children to play instruments. I borrowed an E-flat bass from a friend, I borrowed a slide trombone from another friend, and I purchased a badly-dented second-hand cornet for three dollars and fifty cents. It had an excellent tone. I cleaned and straightened it out as best I could and it worked fine. Then I bought a cheap set of drums and we were in business. I taught them the scales and how to play by note. The children enjoyed it and so did I.

I taught them two pieces of music and they practiced until they got them perfected. At this time I realized that we needed a French horn to complete the harmony portion of the music. I shopped around until I found a badly-dented horn and proceeded to work on it until I got the proper tone in E-flat, which of course went with an E-flat bass. At the time, we lived about one mile from Shawnigan Lake village so the neighbours were unaware of our practice sessions.

One day I saw a notice in the paper of an amateur show to be held in the hall, which was the largest hall on Vancouver Island. I pondered the possibilities. Could I enter my children? I did not want to enter the contest unless we had a chance of winning. After much thought, I decided to enter as The Ward Family Instrumentalists. When I explained it to the official in charge, he began to laugh, and then shouted to two other men, "Hey! Tom wants to enter his kids in the amateur show."

The men regarded my entry as a kind of joke; their high-handed attitude spurred me on to win top honours. On credit, my wife bought a few rolls of crepe paper out of which she made pirouette costumes. The children tried them on and they looked lovely. Perhaps I should mention that in France during World War One, I acted with the First Divisional Concert Party where I conducted bands both onstage and in the open air.

When the contest began, I realized we were up against some stiff talent, as most of the entrants were over sixteen years of age. At last the curtain went down on the last act before ours and while I was assembling the children onstage, the crowd began to leave. I jumped out and shouted, "Ladies and gentlemen! Will you please be seated and listen to the youngest band in the Dominion of Canada."

The people returned to their seats and when they saw the children dressed in their costumes, a tremendous roar went up. We began with "Long, Long Ago," which received a great ovation, and then followed with "Little Brown Jug" in one-step time. When the music ended I knew we had won first prize.

The people of the district knew nothing of our practice so they were overwhelmed. Let me give credit to the children so you will understand what was presented. Marjorie, age twelve, played bass; Jimmy, age eleven, played second cornet; Clara (later Clara Bowden), age nine, played slide trombone; Doris, age seven, French horn; Walter, age five, played drums; Lilly, age four, was conductor, and I managed the solo cornet.

After we won the contest, we were offered a gig in the Duncan Theater for fifteen minutes, at the rate of a dollar a minute. We had one week to prepare so I accepted the offer. Just two days before the show, I received a letter from the man who had loaned us the E-flat bass, he wanted it returned at once as he was leaving town. I sent the instrument on with a friend and then said good-bye to the engagement.

On the way home, an idea struck me; why not use the old organ in place of the E-flat bass? Marjorie could play it instead. Yes, that was it. We could keep our engagement and get that fifteen dollars. We only had one night to practice, so we gave it a try and it was horrible. The organ was in low pitch C, and the other instruments were in E-flat and B-flat. To overcome that, I rewrote their parts one note higher. The organ was still a shade flat, so I pulled the tuning slides out as far as possible. It was still a bit flat, but only a person with musical ability could detect it. The next thing was to get a truck to move the family and instruments to Duncan. Once again we were lucky when the store owner volunteered his truck. We packed the heavy organ down to the light-delivery truck and tried to load it—it was eighteen inches too high. I grabbed a saw and began cutting it off while my wife complained bitterly because it was so beautiful with its carving and glass mirror. I worked feverishly until the saw wouldn't cut anymore, and because of a heavy rainfall, I was sopping wet. I found a long falling saw and put it to work with the truck-driver on one end and me on the other. My only thought was the show must go on.

The top finally came off, but what a terrible mess. My wife covered it with a sheet and we were off to the show. As I sat down beside the driver I found that I was sitting in a pool of water, such was the state of my clothes. I had no change of clothes, so I had to go onstage as I was and hope for the best.

One thing stood in my favour—the audience was so taken with the children that they hardly noticed me. We gave it everything we had and when the final curtain came down I thought the roof was going to come off the place. The children had made a tremendous hit and the manager was delighted. One of the local café owners came backstage and invited us to a big feast and we sure went for it. I think everything in the restaurant was on that table. Many people came to our table and congratulated me on the marvelous job the children had done. It wasn't just the music; it was the sight of those huge instruments in the hands of my little children.

The next day there was a great write-up in the Duncan newspaper and the letters of congratulation started pouring in. Soon we had offers coming in to play at this or that function, and I promised all of them that we would get to them sooner or later.

The next day I decided to go to Victoria to buy a second-hand bass with the fifteen dollars we had earned and on the way I met a salesman who told me he had a Model T two-door sedan for sale in Victoria that was being repainted at the time. There was sixteen dollars owing on it and I could get it for that amount. He also suggested that it would be ideal for my travelling band. We went to look it over and the garage man told me it had many miles left in it. I tried it out and bought it, and then I measured the gas and realized that I didn't have enough to get back to Shawnigan Lake. The mechanic was a nice guy because he gave me a few gallons so I could get home—minus the bass I had started out to get. I told the mechanic about the bass and he suggested that he knew where I might get one; he handed me an address and told me to go there and tell the same story I had told him. With some difficulty I located the house and asked the lady at the door if a Mr. North lived there. She was so nice that I got suspicious. When I glanced about I saw pictures of important people and police officers. I suspected I had bought a stolen car and they were going to arrest me. Then she asked if I would join her in a cup of tea and I agreed. I couldn't understand why she was so nice to me.

As we sat there talking, Mr. North arrived and we were introduced. I told him about my need for a bass and what I was trying to do with the children. For several minutes he appeared in deep

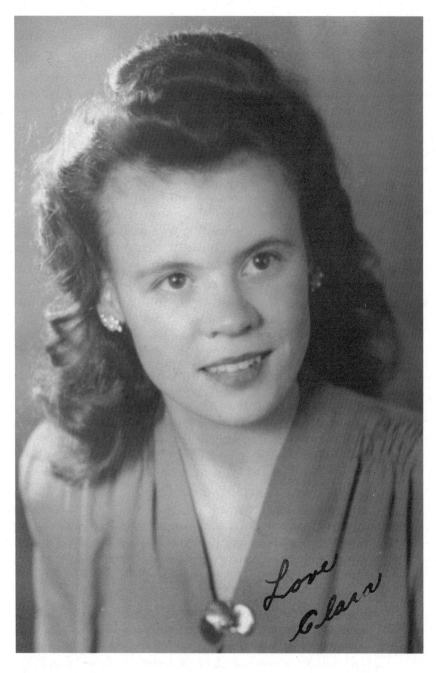

Clara Ward.

thought, and then told me to follow him. We walked downtown and he got me to wait while he went into some music stores. Finally he emerged with a gorgeous silver-plated horn in his hands. The price tag indicated $85 and I knew that it would be worth $250 new. I asked him how I could possibly pay for it and he replied, "This is a gift to your children from the City of Victoria presented by Chief of Police Joe North. And there is just one catch—you have to put on your first concert right here on the street."

I had no trouble promising the first concert to the finest man I have ever met; I firmly believe that if there is a heaven Joe North will be there. All the way home I kept pinching myself to be sure I wasn't dreaming, as I just couldn't believe my luck; I had left home with fifteen dollars and I was returning with a car and a bass horn. When I made the turn into our home, I kept the horn on steady as the children had already arrived home from school. As I pulled into the yard I spotted five or six little heads in the window; when they realized it was Dad, out they came, with a million questions. Then Mother appeared and asked, "Did you spend that money to buy this car?"

Right then Marjorie said, "I didn't want clothes or candy or anything; I just wanted a bass horn." With that she turned toward the house with a forlorn look on her face.

I shouted to her, "Marjorie, look under the back seat!"

She went to the car and then all the children began talking at once. Marjorie ran to her mother and spoke in an excited voice, "Mom, look! I've got a new horn."

Meanwhile, Mother had been sizing me up and finally asked, "Dad, how are we ever going to pay for all this?"

We went into the house and I told them the entire story; this led the children to promise that they would practice hard and play for this wonderful man called Joe North. To further celebrate, all twelve of us piled into the car and went for a ride. We were crammed so tight that I barely had room to drive.

The car began earning its keep the next day when we went to the forest and brought back a large load of fir bark. That evening we sat around a comfortable fire and Mother could not have been happier. After that, I spent every available hour writing music for the children and they worked hard to improve their knowledge and versatility.

Only a few days later I was coming home from work when I noticed one of my sons walking ahead of me. Suddenly he disappeared out of my sight into the brush and I heard him screaming. I ran as quickly as I could to his side and noticed that he had been attacked by a large number of hornets. I shouted at him to run for home and waded right into the hornets to distract them. I stood the attack until he had a headstart and then I ran as fast as possible right into our house. When I took my pants off the hornets rolled out all over the floor; they were everywhere. I killed hornets until the floor looked as if it was covered with axle grease.

That was a terrible time for me. I stayed in bed for a full week; I was swollen everywhere from the neck down. Our neighbours thought it was a great joke, even the doctor laughed his fool head off. It was no joke to me; I was in agony. Some of the lumps were the size of my fist. After I started recovering, I went back to writing music for the band. One week later I had twelve pieces of music ready for rehearsal. The children worked hard and loved it. The main drawing card was three-year-old Lilly who was the conductor, and Walter the drummer. The slide-trombone player, Clara, had a problem—her arms were too short to reach C-sharp, but she managed fine by attaching a piece from a broom stick. One way or another we found a way to get the job done.

Two months later Joe North had us lined up to play on the streets of Victoria. The children were out of school so they would be part of the huge group that lined up to see the Ward Family Tiny Tots Band. We started out with "Blue Danube" and a crowd started forming immediately. Three policemen were busy keeping the crowd back. When the waltz finished the crowd went wild. Two more policemen arrived and the traffic jammed up tight. The police had to alleviate the traffic jam so they moved us to another corner. The crowd followed us and we cut loose with the "Beer Barrel Polka." Ask any policeman that was in the force in 1940; they will never forget it.

When that tune was finished, I thanked the people of Victoria and then Mr. North spoke; he asked the people if they wanted to donate so we could buy more instruments and they readily complied. While he was talking little Lillie was gathering up one, two and five dollar bills. Then Joe got a man to pass the hat while we played yet another tune. Finally Joe North had four men walking around with a blanket to catch donations coming down from the office buildings. What a success; the people were amazed. They were awestruck by such tiny children playing advanced music.

The day was capped when Joe took us to the Hudson's Bay where we had a delicious feast. We showed our appreciation by playing a few more tunes. When we prepared to leave, Joe produced tickets for all of us to the show. I had no keys for the car, but a policeman was standing at the corner so I asked if the car would be safe there. He replied, "Don't worry! No one will steal anything from your car, at least not tonight."

On the way home I stopped to get gas and we counted out the money; it came to $49.16 which was a good sum at that time. When we arrived home intending to surprise Mother, about twelve people were there who had seen the show in Victoria. Mother already knew.

Soon offers began pouring in. We were wanted in Duncan, Courtney, Campbell River, Port Alberni, Cumberland, Nanaimo and other towns along the way. Two months more practice and we were on our way. We first played in Duncan and earned $15.78; our next stop was Courtney where we took in $35; then we walked across the bridge and got another $42.50.

We moved on to Campbell River and played at the dock when the boat came in. People began throwing coins at us, but many of them found their way between the planks and were lost. Then some gentleman loaned us a blanket from his car to catch the coins in. This excited the people and they threw coins until the boat moved away. We showed our appreciation by playing until the boat was out of sight. By that time it had turned cold so I took the family into a café for a hot meal including strawberries and cream. When we got the bill, I almost flipped out; it read, "Compliments of Campbell River." I thanked the proprietor and he wished us the best of luck.

The next day we moved to Cumberland where we found the streets almost deserted. I asked a barber what was going on and he told me that the mine would go off shift at seven o'clock and that we should play on the corner by the bank. Sure enough, as the time rolled around we headed to that corner with a group of youngsters following us. Soon a crowd gathered and we lit out with the "Beer Barrel Polka." We followed that with "Men of Harliech." They encored that piece three times. The collection box tinkled at a steady pace. Bills of all sizes were being tucked into the box. We played a full hour as they danced and filled the streets; we tried to stop but they wanted more and were paying for it. One person came to talk to me and at the same time someone else took all the children for refreshments. Then another gentleman asked me to come for a drink while he appointed someone to watch over the instruments. We went to a bar and he treated me to a glass of beer and a drink of scotch. I felt like a million dollars. This man was obviously some-one of importance, but I never got the chance to find out; he just raved on and on about the band, suggesting that we should tour Canada by taking donations as we travelled. I told him that I liked the idea but I would need a larger vehicle to carry the whole family.

When we returned to the instruments, we saw the band coming down the street followed by a large crowd of children; they were really having a ball. We played on until nine o'clock and then drove

The Ward family band.

back to Courtney for the night. We counted the money which to-
taled $69.25; we could not have been happier. This was far more
money than I received for a whole month on relief. We played for
a while after getting advice from a barber, and we netted $34.65.
Now we were able to start buying more instruments and planning
our Canada-wide trip. My dream was to play on the Major Bowes
Program in the US if such was possible. I also wanted the children
to get much more of an education than they could possibly get in
school.

We continued with our tour of towns in the area and the children got enough exercise to keep them healthy; they also got adequate food that I cooked for them. I had attained the status of
chef by cooking for three hundred men on the construction of
the Grand Trunk Pacific Railway between Edson, AB, and Fort
George, BC, during 1910–14. We finished the tour by playing in
Nanaimo where we took in $48, and then we started the 80 mile
drive toward home. We bought new clothes to look more present-
able to the public and then put the remaining money—$52—away
for our trip.

I worked hard all that winter, saving money and writing music
for the band. By spring we had a repertoire of seventy-five selec-
tions; enough to play for many hours without repetition. Also that
winter, a man named Harry Livingston from Comox, BC, made
me an offer I could not refuse: he would supply his car for a cross-
Canada tour; we simply had to buy his meals and the gas for his
large car. Since there would be thirteen of us, Mother and I would
travel by train with the three tiniest children and meet them in
towns along the way. We made arrangements to leave on May 4,
1940. I was pleased that the band had improved fifty percent over
the winter. This inspired me to purchase new and better instruments for the tour.

The youngest was just a babe-in-arms, so we knew we would
have to use great care regarding drafts and the cold; sickness would
be devastating to our plans. During the last few days at home we
sold most of our possessions to finance the trip; the house was almost empty when we left.

On Saturday morning Mother, I and the three children left by
train for Nanaimo. We booked four rooms in a hotel and I went
to City Hall to see about getting a permit to perform on the street.

Mayor Telford was a fine gentleman who gave us a letter introducing us to mayors and reeves in the cities we would be visiting. He directed me to the police where I got permission to play in Victory Square each evening. That evening we collected sixty dollars. The next day we auditioned in the Orpheum Theatre and then played in front of City Hall. The next day there was a write-up and pictures in the *Vancouver Sun*. The reporters did a great job and told us that they would send the pictures on across Canada. Mr. Ivan Avery got us back two more times to the theatre and paid us well. We played Victory Square through to Saturday and then on Sunday we played in Stanley Park. We intended to play for free, but the good Vancouver citizens treated the children to ice cream and took up collections to help us on our way. The Ward Family Tiny Tots were welcomed with open arms.

We spent eight days in Vancouver and collected three hundred dollars. Then it was on to Chilliwack, where we were not allowed to play in town; we played in a vacant lot with only children in attendance. Our take for the two shows was sixteen cents. We left there way in the hole after paying cabin expenses. Several residents apologized for the treatment we received.

Next on our trip was Boston Bar where we played to a small crowd. The following day we went across the swinging bridge to North Bend and shortly a troop train arrived. We played to the soldiers and one of them requested the "Beer Barrel Polka" and offered $15. He seemed surprised that we were able to play it. Then they all joined in and sang along with the music. We had a great time and earned $20.45; then it was back to Boston Bar where we played but got no collection.

The next day, May 17, we moved to Lytton where a friendly policeman helped set us up; we did very well for such a small town. Then we were off to Ashcroft where we were helped by the nicest and most courteous policemen I have ever met; they couldn't do enough for us. The people were music crazy. After playing on the street, we were invited in to a restaurant where the manager treated us like Hollywood stars. We took a great collection there—$37.42. It was money we certainly needed.

Sunday afternoon found us playing in the park at Kamloops. That evening and the next day we played in the street. The mayor and citizens were so nice to us. What a wonderful town.

On Tuesday we arrived in Vernon where the police refused us permission to play in the centre of town. We played in a few spots but the people only gave us pennies and tin tokens. There wasn't enough money to feed our cats, let alone the price of our cabin. (Little did I know at that time that I would be stationed at Vernon several years later with the guards. I formed a large band and we played around there with great success. The people were okay.)

On May 22, we went to Kelowna and played on the street. Mr. Bouch, the barber was nice to us and gave us an excellent place to play; we did well and I was impressed with this place. We saw a crippled woman playing an accordion and the children rushed to her and gave donations.

We played in Oliver and then went back to Penticton; all told we did quite well. Grand Forks was next on our list and we did alright for a small town. Then we went on to Trail where we found the children and adults so well behaved. The mayor was so kind to us; he gave me a letter written in longhand introducing us to the mayors of cities right through to Regina. Our finances improved considerably.

On May 25 we moved to Rossland where we stayed at the Brooks Auto Camp. We played on the street in the evening and played some hymns which were greatly appreciated. The next day we moved to Trail where we met some wonderful people and made expenses.

We crossed on a ferry on May 28, 1940, and made our way into Nelson where we found the people so well behaved; at the request of the mayor and population we stayed over and played the next day. The mayor wrote a beautiful handwritten letter of introduction to the mayors of the other cities we were to visit; he also took an instant liking to the children. Our finances had improved to the point that we had no worries.

May 30 found us in Cranbrook where the town elders made us welcome. I could tell by meeting the town leaders what to expect and it proved true in this case. We played in front of the King Edward Hotel and in the school festival. The people were extremely generous. This ended our tour of BC.

The Alberta town of Blaremore was next on our tour. We played there for two evenings and then played at Coleman and Belview. We returned to Blaremore and played another gig and we did well monetarily. What a fine town!

Lethbridge was next on our list; we played there for two days. The police were so polite and the people greatly enjoyed the music. We did so well that I bought the children new clothes and shoes, which were fast wearing out from all the travel.

On June 5 we arrived by train and car at Medicine Hat where I met the Principle of the Redcliff School. He was with me in the 5th Battalion Infantry in France. We had a lot to talk about and he helped us a great deal; we did well dollar-wise.

On June 6 we arrived in Maple Creek, Saskatchewan. What a jolly lot of people. The police moved us to a bigger area because the people went wild over the little tots with such big instruments. The drummer was only five and Clara on the trombone at eight simply drove them wild. The police were so helpful; one officer had been with me in the war and he graciously donated ten dollars to help with our tour. He took me in for some stiff refreshments while the children were eating ice cream donated by a store. We had such a wonderful time; good luck Maple Creek.

Then we were on to Swift Current where the lady of the camp we stayed at told me that they had an excellent band of their own. I asked a few questions and realized that I knew three members of the band, as we had played together with the 5th Battalion in France. I asked her to phone them and tell them that Buckeye was in town, which she did. I had earned the stage-name of Buckeye while serving in France.

As soon as they got the word, they rushed right down. We had a great time reminiscing and they promised to bring their sixty-piece band out on the street Monday evening for a concert, with all proceeds to go to our tour. We played for a few days and when the concert started we set up our little band in front of their band. They led with "O'Canada" and they really had a fantastic band. When we played the "Beer Barrel Polka," they gave us a standing ovation, probably because of the little children. The bandmaster got a tremendous kick out of watching the four-year-old con-ductress leading the band. We did so well there. Thank you Swift Current; we will never forget you.

Our next stop was Regina—the town I had been warned against by several mayors. My first impulse was to go right through it, but then I remembered that we had not given up in the war, so why not give it a go? It didn't take long for me to realize that the advice I had received concerning Regina was right on the money.

I asked a policeman who to see to get permission to play on the street. He sent me to a Colonel, all in uniform and important looking; I figured he was a retired English Army Officer. I showed him my introductory letters and asked permission. Instantly he exploded, "We don't want a bunch of kids with tin whistles making a racket around here; I could have you arrested. Better get out of town as soon as possible."

I thanked him and left, but not out of town. Instead I went to the local radio station where I met a Mr. Al Thoults who was in

Clara with her husband Hap in later years.

charge of the Army and Navy Program. We played a tune for him and he hired us to do a half-hour show for the Army and Navy store. We were to be well paid.

We played for twenty-five minutes and then I spoke. I told the public how we had been rejected by the police and apologized for not meeting them in person. After the show, I received the following letter from the radio station:

> To Whom It May Concern,
> This letter acknowledges an appearance as guest artists on the Army and Navy Stores program of golden memories—Canada's oldest continuous radio program. The Ward Family Orchestra of Vancouver, BC—en-route to New York City—broadcasted a half-hour program over radio station CKCK. This program met with immediate response from a large listening audience, including long-distance telephone calls and telegrams which testified to the popularity of this band. We would be honored to present this band to the people of Saskatchewan on some future date. We sincerely recommend them to any organization or group desiring the finest in entertainment. May we add our best wishes for the success of this family in their worthy endeavors and wish them God speed in their climb to success in the radio world.
>
> Yours sincerely, W. N. Thultz,
> Director of Programs

We were amply paid by the Army and Navy and so, Mr. Colonel, what about your tin whistles? I found deep satisfaction in the realization that all the people around Regina were not music dead.

Our next stop was Indian Head and then Whitewood. On to Kennedy where we saw the rodeo on June 15, and then back to Whitewood where we played for the Red Cross. We did well in all these towns. That was end of our tour of Saskatchewan.

June 17, we arrived in Virden, Manitoba where we slept in tents because there were no cabins available. We played in the street and did well—which means we were able to pay our way. Next on our journey came Portage LaPrairie. It was so cold that we found it difficult to play. We did our best and made our expenses. Then it was on to Winnipeg where I couldn't get permission to play in the city. We played in a market square, out from the centre of town. A policeman came to me and demanded to know who I was. One would think we were escaped prisoners. We played two days on the streets and made ten and twelve dollars respectively.

We played in St. Bonifice for the Catholic Old-Man's Home and then for the orphans, and it was much appreciated. The next day we got involved in an accident. We just crossed a streetcar track when we were side-swiped by a Model T car with inoperable brakes. It hit my side and although I was shaken up, I told the police that I would not pursue charges as the man was poor. My only thought was that the show must go on, which it did.

Because of the accident we were out of wheels. This forced us to stay in Winnipeg for a while to earn some money. As it turned out, we bought a 1929 Packard car that was in good shape. We gave the garage what was left of our Plymouth and $150 to boot. This vehicle was perfect, because now we could all travel together and save the train fares. It seemed the accident was a godsend. The only downside was that tires were worn so we had to drive with great care until we earned the money to buy new ones.

We drove to Kenora on June 28 only to find the campgrounds were full; this forced us to camp in a farmer's field. The Mounted Police were polite and sincere gentlemen. We played Friday and Saturday and did really well; the money was sorely needed. The crowds in Kenora kept asking us to play "There'll Always Be an England." I didn't have the music for it but I borrowed a copy that had the wrong timing. I sat up most of the night rewriting it and when we played it, people loved it. One man asked me for a copy for his band and I loaned it to him. I never got it back, so I had to write it all over again. While in Kenora we took a boat ride on Lake of the Woods and played on a tour boat trip to the Thousand Islands. The scenery was stunning and the trip was educational for my family.

On Monday we headed for Fort Francis but only went twenty

miles before we got a flat tire; I bought a second-hand tire from a nearby garage and we were off again. We only got fifteen miles out of that tire before it blew. We camped beside the road and found that there was no garage within miles; this forced us to patch the tire and carry on. We drove slowly for thirty-five miles and got another flat tire. On July 3 we reached the town of Emo and got another flat tire, but this was fixed in a garage. Strange as it seems, all the flats occurred on the same back wheel. That evening we played for a ball game and later we played in the city where we got good coin. The local baker came to our cabin with bread and buns; another man brought us butter and eggs. We played two sessions because the people were so good to us.

On July 5 we drove to Fort Francis and played with the Legion Band; all donations went to us. The Legion women came to our cabin to see that baby and mother were doing fine; they looked after us as if we were their own. Saturday evening we played and took in forty dollars. On Sunday we went to Reef Point and played for a church and later the Boy Scouts. At their insistence we had dinner with them. When we arrived back at our cabins, we started playing and the circus nearby complained that we were taking their crowd away. Someone went and turned off the lights so we had to stop playing. A group of citizens took control and got the lights put on again in thirty minutes. Word got around and soon we had a huge crowd and no one was at the circus. Soon the circus manager came and asked me if we would play on the grounds so he could get some business. He promised the children could go on all the rides for free. We took him up on the offer and the children had a joyful time. That evening we played again and "There'll Always Be an England" and the "Beer Barrel Polka" were their favourites. The next two nights we took in a total of ninety dollars.

On July 15 we attempted to cross the US border to visit New York and get on Major Bowes Radio Program. We were refused entry on the grounds that we didn't have enough money and they were concerned we would become a public charge.

We changed our plans and decided to return home by a different route. One evening a hall owner hired us to play for two hours. The hall was packed. He was so pleased that he gave us sixty dollars for two hours; what a pleasant surprise that was. Another time we just finished playing when a man walked up to me and said I had played a copyrighted tune without permission and if I didn't give him fifteen dollars he would sue me. I asked what tune it was and he told me it was a tune I had composed called "Moonlight on the Fraser." I told him to get lost or I would call the police. That did it, I never saw him again.

We worked our way back west until we reached Redcliff, Alberta, where a glass factory was being constructed. My two oldest children and I got jobs there so we stayed all winter and into the next summer. We had left Vancouver with ten dollars and an old car. Soon we owned our own home and I went to work for the Veterans Guards. We continued playing for weddings, dances, picnics and wherever music was needed. Music has been my life.

Author's note: Thomas Ward wrote this story, which was passed on to me by his daughter Clara—the eight-year-old slide trombone player. She went on to become an inspiration to other women by becoming a guide, trapper and prospector in the Quesnel area of BC. She and her husband Hap Bowden were the source of my book, *Wilderness Dreams*.

WOLVES
& HORSES

I believe that wolves are the smartest and most intriguing animal in the forest. People who have listened to the howls of a pack of thirty or more wolves have stated that it was a sound they never forgot. Even many years later they just had to close their eyes to recall one of the most impressive sounds in nature.

A little over half a century ago many woodsmen attempted to earn their livelihood hunting wolves for their bounty and pelts. I say *attempted*, because often the results were a complete failure. Retired trapper and guide Glen Hooker of Dome Creek, BC, knew what it was like to hunt wolves for weeks on end without getting a glimpse of them.

One of Glen's favourite wolf stories concerned his deceased brother Lawrence who trapped the Keg Creek area near Pass Lake. Lawrence was a tough kid who, at the tender age of fifteen, spent fifty-three days alone in that remote wilderness area without seeing another human. He trapped for one entire winter living in a large, hollow log with a husky dog for companionship and a campfire out front for cooking and warmth.

In an effort to cash-in on the bounty money, these two brothers pursued a wolf pack along the Torpy River for several weeks during a winter in the forties. On some trips they would snowshoe downriver from Pass Lake, and other times they would snowshoe upriver from the mouth of the Torpy River; this meant that the wolves never knew what direction they would come from and so it improved their chances of success.

Glen described to me that the wolves were so intelligent that they would not step on their snowshoe trails. Instead they would take a mighty leap through the air and land on the opposite side without touching their path. Were the wolves trying to avoid traps that were set along the trail? Glenn states that they never set any traps on their trails, suggesting that the wolves were cautious to the point of being ridiculous. On the other hand, the wolves came to their cabin while they were away and even peed on their splitting block right beside the cabin door. It appears obvious they were making their claim to the area.

One winter day the two men surprised the wolves and got away several shots. Three wolves went down and another managed to run a short distance where it crawled down into the snow beside a big tree. Lawrence went back to their cabin and returned with a shovel, then spent a lot of time trying to dig the creature out. When that failed, he built a huge fire on top of the snow and waited as it slowly melted down into the three metres (ten feet) of snow. At last Lawrence gave up on the fire and crawled in after the wolf. He had a .22 pistol in one hand which was less than useless because the barrel was shot. When he got close to the wolf, he fired some shots but all he got was some growls in return. Once again Lawrence went to the cabin and returned with his rifle. He lit his bug (candle in a can), and crawled down into the hole again with the bug in one hand and a big stick in the other. When he tapped the wolf with the stick to check if it was dead, the wolf left a set of heavy-duty teeth marks in the stick. With no other option left, Lawrence crawled back out and got his rifle. When he got back down in the hole again he fired the rifle which blew out the candle in the bug. Once again he came out from under the tree, lit the light and gave it another try. The moral of the story was that they got the wolf, but they sure earned every cent they got from the bounty on that creature.

During the winter of 1950–51, I was employed as a section hand for the Canadian National Railway. At that same time, a Penny resident named Ed Chambers decided to have a go at bounty hunting. Several times that winter we picked him up with our motor car and gave him a ride back home. At times we would meet him along the railway after he had walked on snowshoes for perhaps eight or ten kilometres. His favourite trick was to follow the riverbank and hope to catch them out on the ice where he had a chance to get away several shots before they reached cover. Although he made many trips that winter, he never got a shot at a wolf. I recall the time we picked him up with our motor car and I asked him if he was having any luck. His reply was brief, "Them buggers got eyes and ears in both ends."

~

My nephew, Dwayne Proctor, spent several years running snow-plows on the logging roads north of Babine Lake and consequently had abundant opportunities to study wolves and their interactions with moose. Often he was the first to drive the roads after fresh snow had fallen; this left a roadmap that was interesting to study. Some of the packs were up to fifteen in number and many times he noted that these packs made a 120-kilometre (75-mile) tour of their respective areas in one week. When the wolves did cut a fresh moose track, the hunt was on and they would pursue it to its obvious conclusion. On one occasion he found where a large wolf had been killed by a moose. An open gash in the wolf's chest showed that it had probably been caught by a sharp antler. The moose escaped that time, but about one week later the pack returned and took the moose down. As Dwayne put it, "It seems that once they made a decision to take a moose down, the end result proved they were successful."

Several times on fresh snowfall Dwayne noted where two packs had met on the road and for about two kilometres (one mile) the roadway was a solid mass of wolf tracks. Almost as if they were deliberately meeting and spending time together. This usually took place in January and February when wolves are heading into and during their mating season. Could it be that this is where and when they undergo a change of leadership? Perhaps this is when and how the larger packs introduce new alpha males and, as a by product, introduce new blood into the packs. As an elderly trapper asked me back in 1964, "Is it just coincidence that a lone wolf appears toward spring, following a few days behind the packs, picking up scraps? Dome Creek trapper Arne Jenson felt that these lone straggler wolves were deposed leaders who had been forced out of office and into exile.

Dwayne echoes many others who state that wolves are exceptionally intelligent creatures and points out that countless times he has been right close to them but for the most part, never sees them.

Another story that involved wolves was told to me by John Conway who was just a teenager when it took place. During the autumn of 1958 guide Anund Hansen was prepared to take hunters into the Pass Lake area near the McGregor River. In late September he met the group of hunters at the Prince George airport and was going to take them by floatplane into Pass Lake where he kept his pack horses. This saved countless miles of travel as he kept his horses right in his guiding territory at Pass Lake. Bad luck took over at that point when a snowstorm moved through the area and dumped a half metre (two feet) of snow which prevented the plane from flying. After a few days of continuous snowfall Anund gave up on the trip and the hunters returned home to the US empty-handed.

As time passed, Anund became worried about the welfare of the horses so he got his brother Jimmy and friend John Conway to travel to the end of the Pass Lake Road. From there they had to snowshoe back to his camp to find the horses and hopefully lead them back home for the winter. With a steady snowstorm in progress, it didn't take long for the two lads to get lost. From November 8–20, the two young men wandered around in the forest until they finally found some blaze marks on trees. The obvious question is, "Why didn't the men backtrack?" The answer is that the snow kept drifting and burying their trails.

They followed the blaze marks which led them out to Walter Sande's trapline cabin at Pass Lake. After a short search they found two of the horses. They led the horses back to the logging camp about eleven kilometres (seven miles) distant where they met the logging boss Ray Mueller. As it turned out, Ray had problems of his own which he quickly related to them. That afternoon, he had been hunting caribou with his young son Don. Several hours later Ray arrived at their agreed-to meeting spot, but Don was not there. Ray made a large campfire and cut a supply of wood for Don, and then headed back toward home with his pick-up truck to get help. Jimmy and John readily agreed to lend their assistance, but stated that first they needed some food. Ray drove them to his home in Sinclair Mills where his wife Louisa plied them with food and a stiff drink of hot rum for a chaser.

Armed with a rifle, a gas lantern, and a dog, they returned to the campfire to find Don sitting on a log staring into the fire. Around him in the forest a large pack of wolves set up a chorus that would have sent shivers down the spines of adults, let alone a teenager who had been turned around in the forest and had back-tracked his snowshoe trail to the campfire meeting spot. Assuming that Don had spotted the approaching gas lantern, the men failed to announce their arrival. Instead, the dog they had brought along ran right up to Don, who instantly mistook it for a wolf. According to John it is enough to say that Don probably aged a few years in a matter of a few seconds that evening.

As for the remaining horses that were left near Pass Lake, Don Mueller went back and found two of them terribly chewed up by wolves so he shot them. The other horses were found by trapper/guide Walter Sande. They were in pathetic condition. Anund's father, Ole Hansen, told me that when Walter found them, two had been killed by wolves. The others had been eating devil's clubs and were in such pathetic condition that he mercifully put them out of their misery.

~

I recall another wolf story that began the winter day around 1975 when a plane buzzed above our home at Penny. About an hour later the phone rang and my friend Vic Litnosky informed me that it had been him that had buzzed my house with a Cessna 185 aircraft he had just purchased. He also told me that he had spotted three wolves eating a moose carcass three kilometres (two miles) downriver from Penny. He was extremely interested in having a close look at the kill, so a couple hours later we were on snowmobiles heading to the kill. By the time we arrived the wolves had evaporated into the surrounding forest, but the attack on the moose was evident by the trail in the snow. The wolves had driven the moose down a steep hill onto the river ice, one on each side and one directly behind. As soon as they reached the ice, they attacked and the moose was brought down less than fifty metres (164 feet) from the hill. Although young and healthy, the cow moose didn't stand a chance.

We looked the situation over and enjoyed the beautiful winter day for a while and Vic asked how thick I thought the river ice was. I guessed a foot or two and then offered to find out. I took the axe I always carried on the snowmobile and struck the ice, only to have it go through with one stroke. I pushed it down the length of the handle and didn't touch any more ice. I glanced at Vic only to see his face go white; as I'm sure mine was too. Without a word we fired up our machines and didn't look back until we were off the river. There had been less than a finger length of ice beneath us. Perhaps the reader can understand why I never again went out on the river ice with my snowmobile. Had we broke through the ice into the fast river current it would have meant certain death for both of us.

~

Woodsmen in the northern reaches of British Columbia and the Yukon often tell stories of moose wintering in herds of between fifty and one hundred. On a few occasions I have seen pictures to support these claims. While I am not familiar with moose bunching up in such large numbers in the Interior of BC, I know others who swear that they do. My personal experience is that moose bunch up in large numbers while they wait for rivers to freeze over so they can cross to their winter feeding grounds. In fact, I have seen pictures of up to fifty moose at the Hansard Bridge waiting for the river ice to freeze so they could make their way to the Bowron River wintering grounds.

Wilf Howlett of Prince George tells an interesting moose/wolf story. One winter day in the late fifties he met game warden Milt Warren near the Parsnip River north of Prince George and Milt invited him to come along on a snowshoe trip. They walked a few miles to where a herd of about seventy moose were gathered near the river. As they neared the moose, they came upon a well-tramped wolf trail that completely encircled the herd. What an easy winter that wolf pack must have enjoyed. Although the men didn't hang around the area, it is a good bet that the wolf pack just drove a moose out of the bunch as needed, and then rested up and repeated the procedure without any amount of effort wasted on travel through deep snow drifts.

Wilf had another interesting adventure regarding wolves that took place while he was employed as cat skinner (tractor operator) near Reid Lake north of Prince George back in the sixties. One day two fallers asked him to accompany them to where they were falling because they had something of interest to show him. When they arrived at the site, they found three dead wolves and one dead moose. The abundant sign showed that there had been ten wolves in the pack and one had been caught by the moose's antlers and thrown up into a tree where it remained draped over some thick branches. The other two wolves had been trampled deep into the snow. It was obvious that the wolves had eventually won the fight, because most of the moose carcass had been devoured by then. Wilf added that there were several balls of moose hair strewn about that the wolves had coughed out. Most important to me, is that I'm sure this is the only time I have heard of more than one wolf getting killed in a battle with moose.

I doubt that one can find a more controversial subject than whether wolves attack people or not. The last few years several cases have been acknowledged and yet some people will not accept it as fact. On November 6, 2007, the Prince George *Citizen* carried the following:

> Prince Albert, Sask.—A coroner's jury has decided that it was wolves, not a bear, that attacked and killed an Ontario man in a remote mine site in northern Saskatchewan. The partially eaten body of Kenton Carnegie, twenty-two, was found November 8, 2005, about a half kilometre from Points North Landing, about 750 kilometres northeast of Saskatoon. The jury deliberated for about four hours before handing down its decision that Carnegie died from "injuries consistent to that of a wolf attack."

The article ended by stating that wolf attacks are increasing all over Canada. It pointed out that where wolves are protected they have lost their fear of man.

~

There are a great many stories of horses being attacked by wolves. Yet the Jenson brothers of Dome Creek, BC, raised colts back in the McGregor Mountains and not once did they have a problem with wolves. On the other hand, Skook Davidson lost eighteen head of horses in one winter to wolves in the Kechika River area. What is one to make of this apparent contradiction? Apparently the answer lies in whether they get a taste of horsemeat. If they get started they will not quit because they find the meat delicious. A rancher told me that if he loses a horse to accident or disease he immediately burns or buries it. He does not want wolves to get even a taste, because if they do, they will return.

I know of several cases where horses were attacked because they were abandoned in the woods by their owners, abandonment being a fairly common event over half a century ago. In bygone days it was often difficult to get horses out of the mountains when surprised by heavy, early snowfalls. One guide attempted to drop hay for his stranded horses from an aircraft, but fearing that the bales may hit the horses and injure them, he made the drop too far from the horses. Either the horses didn't see the bales falling, or else they were too weak to get to them. The outcome was pitiful as the horses slowly starved to death. This individual told me that this tragedy took place in the forties. He also explained that he had

Tim and Monica Brown digging a trench in an attempt to rescue the trapped horses.

gone through enough and asked that I not reveal his identity. He closed the matter by saying that he was so sickened by the whole thing that he never used horses again.

As stated, it was often difficult to get feed to stranded horses many years ago, but that should not be an excuse in these days of helicopters and snowmobiles. Yet, sad to say, it still happens.

Just this past Christmas season two McBride residents on snowmobiles were searching for an overdue rider when they came upon two abandoned horses in the Renshaw snowmobiling area north of McBride. Logan Jeck and Leif Gunster were shocked to find what they thought were two moose suddenly become horses. Over the next several days a supply of water and a limited amount of food was brought to the animals so they wouldn't overeat. Attendants did what they could by bringing blankets to the horses to protect them from the cold. Then a massive rescue program got underway. Fighting through two metres (seven feet) of snow in minus thirty degrees Celsius temperatures, a hardy group of individuals shovelled a trail for one kilometre (half a mile) to where a packed snowmobile trail existed. It took an additional seven hours to walk the horses to a horse trailer, a distance of twenty-eight kilometres (seventeen miles).

Jeck stated that because of the extreme cold the snow refused to pack. This meant that the volunteers had to shovel almost to ground level. Thankfully a total of about forty people chipped in at some point or in some way to make the outcome a success. Kudos to all, I say. Is it my imagination or do rural people make themselves available to help each other much more than their city opposites? In due course, the horses were brought to McBride where they were cared for pending a hearing into the whole matter.

Dave Jeck guides Belle through the trench.

Volunteers shovelled a one kilometre trail in minus 30 degree celsius. Birgit Stutz and Monica Brown take a well-earned rest.

One view of the entire debacle was expressed in a letter to the
Prince George *Citizen* by Dunster (near McBride) resident Birgit
Stutz who was involved in the rescue:

> The man who abandoned two horses in the Renshaw
> area to die of starvation wants them back. Frank
> Mackay, a lawyer from Edmonton, said he made two
> attempts to retrieve the animals and made "every effort
> possible" to save them.
>
> I am appalled. Volunteers spent a week freeing the
> emaciated, trapped horses under extreme weather con-
> ditions, and he expects to just get them back.
>
> I am not blaming Mckay for losing his horses or get-
> ting into trouble in the backcountry. Things like that
> happen. However, not putting in more effort to find the
> animals and, when he finally did locate them, leaving
> them for dead, to me is completely unacceptable.
>
> Mckay abandoned his two pack horses on September
> 12 after hitting rough terrain and didn't come back to

look for them until the last week in October because he was too busy. What about the time of the volunteers, who put their lives on hold to rescue the two horses? Is his time more valuable than everybody else's?

And why didn't Mckay ask locals for help to find his horses? He definitely had enough time to do so, and it would have been a lot easier to get the horses out of the mountains before the snow hit, and while the animals were still in decent condition.

Mackay said he doubts locals would have helped a stranger. Well, he didn't even try, and seeing how the community came to the rescue of the two horses, I beg to differ. When Mackay eventually did locate the horses, he left them to die a slow, agonizing death by starvation. Mackay claims he didn't go up the mountain to kill the horses and that he didn't have a gun. That may be so, but that is still no excuse to "let nature take its course."

As well, Mackay's lack of participation in the rescuing of the horses shows a complete lack of commitment. Where was he when the rescue mission was underway? Mackay claims he was too injured to participate. I am sure he could have helped out in other ways—informing sledders [snowmobile riders] down at the parking lot about the rescue effort, providing hot drinks for the volunteers or buying them supper.

I think I can speak for the majority of the volunteers that we don't want to see these horses returned to Mackay. He abandoned the two equines, giving up ownership, and left them to die. They are no longer his.

The amount of raw emotion in the letter is obvious, and rightfully so. At last word, the SPCA has taken control of the animals and state that they will not be returned. As of February 24, I have received word that Mr. Mackay has been charged with three counts of cruelty to animals. Two counts under the Criminal Code of Canada, and one count under the Prevention of Cruelty to Animals Act. If convicted, he faces a maximum fine of ten thousand dollars and up to five years in jail. He also faces a prohibition on owning animals.

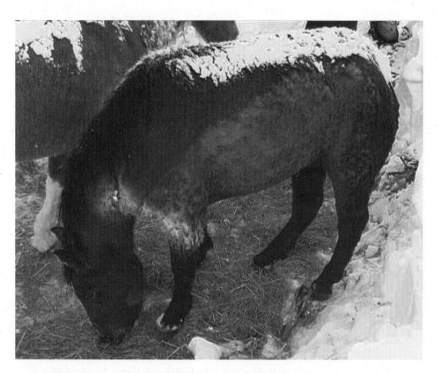

After almost five weeks without food Belle needed rescue.

In my humble opinion, it is often ignorance that allows these things to happen. If a person had any idea how much agony horses go through when they are left to starve, then I find it difficult to believe they could willingly let it happen.

The most extreme case ever to come to my attention occurred in a heavy snowbelt area east of Prince George. Two months passed before the snow settled and the owner found his horses. The only vegetation protruding above the snow was willow bushes and devil's club, and you guessed it, the horses attempted to eat some devil's club. One of the horses had a half-metre (two-foot) piece of caught in his throat and was continually convulsing. I realize that this not a pretty story, nor is it meant to be. When we consider the amount of work these animals perform for their owners, surely it is not too much to expect some tender loving care in return.

One guide explained that pack horses are trained to stay near the spot where they are let loose to graze. It should be no wonder that the Renshaw horses didn't wander down to lower elevations as the owner had hoped for. For some strange reason domesticated horses will starve even when there is an abundance of food in their general area, as noted by men such as Frank Cooke who worked for Skook Davidson for years in the Kechika Valley. Frank stated that Skook repeatedly made him drive the horses to new range, if he didn't, then the horses would stay in an area where they had tramped the snow until it was frozen hard. He said that in general they wouldn't move to where the meadows were not tramped unless they were driven. Frank added that wild horses instinctively know this and frequently move to where they can paw (or perhaps I should use the word "hoof") up new feed.

True lovers of horses take great care to see that they winter in good shape. Skook Davidson, who packed and guided in the north for many years, spent most of his income hiring planes to ferry in oats for his up to two hundred head of horses.

Another story of a true horse lover was told to me by pilot Don Redden of Prince George. In 1971 a guide hired him to fly a ton of hay into the Nazko area, west of Quesnel, because he had not been able to get his horses out before the heavy snow came. Don took the door off a Twin Otter and the guide fired a few bales of hay out on every pass. About a month later the guide checked the horses again and was not satisfied with their condition. He then hired a tractor to punch an access road into the area and followed it with a truck load of feed.

In closing this chapter on wolves and horses, I must make the point that for me horses represent the mountains like nothing else I know of. A pack train in the high country is a thing of beauty in my opinion. But then I have always been biased where mountains are concerned. I spent so many wonderful years around the timberline. If one were to ask me what my favourite memories are of the mountains I would have to state that the endless sounds of nature impressed me the most. Of all the sounds of the woods, my favourites are the mournful howls of a large pack of wolves and the cry of loons. As I have stated before, they bring out the true meaning of the word "wild" in wilderness. They are sounds that one never forgets. As for the most memorable sights, it has to be mother and cub grizzlies; especially when they are play fighting. It almost seems impossible to believe that something so wild and at times ferocious can at the same time seem so playful and gentle.

One of my favourite poets of the wild places has to be Brian Salmond of Dawson Creek, BC. In among his many poems is one that really touches on horses and wolves and the reality of nature. Brian writes from his heart and when that is coupled with his years of experience with horses and mountains, such as the five years he spent guiding for Lynn Ross, it surely shines through in his writing. With his permission I enter the following poem and hope my readers enjoy it as much as I have:

WINTERING OUT

The drenching August rains make way for September's killing frosts,
And in their wakes are buried by October's snow and lost.
The waning of the season brings the duty it entails
De-louse all the pack strings, pull the shoes and check for nails.

Now watch for scalds and cinch galls and check them close for sores.
Cut back the lame and thin ones and a team to hitch for chores.
Swing wide the main gate at the pens and set the leaders free
Then head them west to winter out until spring grants liberty

For it's tough out there with the wild things when snow is belly deep
And crystal snow is hard to paw to find the grass that's asleep.
And the cold like no one knows it, presents its savage bite
That drains the strength but sparks the need to forage through the night.

At forty some below the northern nights that hiss and sway
The river locked in silence waits the journey on its way
The grinding, moaning shore ice as it shoves against the grain
And trees that pop like pistol shots as its heartwood feels the strain

The flats along the river are hemmed with misty haze
Where the slough grass waits a victim of a hungry equine graze.
The frost-rimmed nostrils exit steam like a locomotive's stack
And the shaggy manes are wind-torn, ice is caked along their backs

Through a broken jack pine snag the wind is screaming in their ears
And every head is jerked alert, each heart beats hard in fear.
Thev've heard the call a thousand times from a savage, heartless beast
For lobo and his mangy pack are out to strike a feast.

Then through the fingers of the moon the devil's dogs appear
The slinking shadows of their forms, grotesque as they draw near.
Like spiders trained they watch and wait for fate to deal its blow
Just one mistake, a single chance is all it takes you know.

The lead mare snorts, her nerves on edge, she knows where she's at
She'll play her cards and stand her ground, until her hand is pat.
But not so with them all, there was one that chanced to run.
A barn-raised flatland creature that had lived its dying sun.

His final sprint has ended in a spray of flying snow and ice
Hacked down by canine ivory, like a sharpened hatchet's slice.
The law of the land is witnessed and the strong will eat their fill
Cause this is how it's always been and I suppose it always will.

In the gray light of the morning in its undertaker's role
The raven views the grisly scene from its perch upon a pole.
In high hopes he announces to all his feathered friends
"Come join the feast, another nag has met its dismal end."

And then there is the foolhardy that choose to graze up high
Where the wind-swept grass is sparse and timber meets the sky.
By mid-stream winter their grass is gone and so is their descent
They fight the deep and drifted snow until their strength is spent.

The last few days of the second month there comes a short reprieve
The southwest winds blow strong and loud and cause the cold to leave.
It takes away the cutting edge and softens up the snow
And melts a ring of promise around the stumps and rocks that show

Then the cold returns, retains its grip and makes it hard to paw
The frozen crust of glassy ice that cuts the pasterns raw.
And then it's over – the high suns of March warm the valley floors
Send the creeks and rivers on their way to distant shores.

The brood mare stands and soaks the sun into her shedding hide.
And her flank beats out in patience of the growing life inside.
For like the wild things existing as a link in nature's chain.
The fact that she has beat the odds will be her biggest gain.

From ancestor to descendant through the wisdom of this mare,
Genetics and passing time ensure survival traits are there.
And spring will bring a new birth from a mother's heart so stout
But the playful foal won't even know his mother wintered out.

~

When I think about the wild places, as I often do, I recall a view expressed so well by another man who spent fifty years guiding and trapping. People that have read my book *Wilderness Dreams* will recall Hap Bowden's three-month search for gold through Northern BC in 1947. In his diary he made it plain that the wolves impressed him a great deal. In turn, after he finished the trip he put his strongest feelings into a short poem that truly touched me:

This is solitude and yet;

a world of beauty—a land we can't forget.

Where nature beckons within our souls we bless,

a spot of freedom in God's loneliness.

I doubt that there could ever be a better definition of the wilderness.

COURTESY STAN SIMPSON

Acknowledgements

Once again I wish to thank the Bob Harkins branch of the Prince George Public Library for their endless assistance, also Bob Campbell and The Exploration Place for copies of pictures from the long ago.

Others who have helped in this endeavor are Joan West, Maxine Koppe, Cherry Corless, Birgit Stutz, Marie Moffat, David Humphreys, Allen Spoklie, Trevor Higham, Al Thorpe, Elmer Micks, George Storm, Charlie Bertschi, Vern Gogolin, Bob van Somer, Jack Corless, Steve and Rod Marynovich, Jay Sherwood, Kristina Stark, Bob Campbell, Brian Salmond and John Perry—who spent endless hours recalling almost a century of adventure on a ranch east of Prince George.

—Jack Boudreau